MIKAEL KROGERUS
ROMAN TSCHÄPPELER

THE RULES BOOK

44 PRINCIPLES TO MASTER WORKING LIFE

Translated from the German by Gesche Ipsen

Also by Mikael Krogerus & Roman Tschäppeler and available from Profile Books:

The Change Book

The Collaboration Book

The Decision Book

The Get Things Done Book

The Question Book

The Test Book

The Rules Book

CONTENTS

Foreword 1

Part 1. How to Survive Meetings, Deadlines and Other Workplace Adventures 5
The Ketchup Effect 6
Sturgeon's Law 10
Parkinson's Law 14
The 333 Method 18
Hofstadter's Law 20
Plotz's Law 24
The Pareto Principle 28
Parkinson's Law of Triviality 32
Brooks' Law 36
Goodhart's Law 40
The Locksmith's Paradox 44
Murphy's Law 48

Part 2. When You're Convinced You Should Be Doing Everything Differently 53
Chesterton's Fence 54
Amara's Law 58
The KISS Principle 62
Sutton's Law 66
Strummer's Law 70
The Canada Principle 72
The Law of Unintended Consequences 74
The IKEA Effect 78
The MAYA Principle 80
Lindy's Law 84

Part 3. Understanding Yourself (and Others) Better ... 89

Wiio's Law ... 90

The Peter Principle ... 94

Jaspers' Law ... 98

Brach's Law ... 102

The Law of the Comfort Zone ... 106

The Region-Beta Paradox ... 110

The Goldilocks Principle ... 114

The Big-Fish-Little-Pond Effect ... 118

The Clothes-Chair Principle ... 120

Part 4. How to Handle Life's Big Questions ... 123

Morrison's Laws ... 124

Pascal's Wager ... 126

Occam's Razor ... 128

Agnes Allen's Law ... 132

Korzybski's Law ... 136

The Law of Two Sides ... 140

The 1 Per Cent Rule ... 142

Laver's Law of Fashion ... 144

The Popsicle Test ... 146

The Tocqueville Effect ... 148

The One-Step-Closer Rule ... 152

The 10-10-10 Method ... 154

Epilogue ... 157

Box's Law ... 158

More Rules ... 162

Appendix ... 165

Sources ... 166

About the Authors ... 170

Acknowledgements ... 171

FOREWORD:
RULES – THE LONG AND SHORT OF THEM

We have long relied on science to uncover the laws of nature – such as those governing gravity and thermodynamics, or the order of mathematical operations. But whereas Newton's law of universal gravitation explains beyond reasonable doubt why ketchup drips from your burger, unfortunately it doesn't tell us why it happens every time you're wearing a white shirt. That would be Murphy's law: if something can go wrong, it will.

Murphy's law is an unwritten rule. You may not find it mentioned in any textbook, but its impact is unavoidable. The effects of unwritten rules can't always be *proved* – but they can be *felt*. They encapsulate something deeply familiar. They correspond with life experience rather than academic theories. And they describe the internal logic of modern (working) life better than any degree in psychology ever could.

The so-called ketchup effect – *nothing happens for a long time, and then everything happens all at once* – is obviously not a law of nature as such, but still, we've all experienced it at some point. Or take Agnes Allen's law – *almost anything is easier to get into than out of.* Does it apply to everything? No, of course not. But if you've ever tried to cancel a mobile phone contract or end a complicated relationship, you'll know that Agnes Allen was on to something fundamental, universal even.

Some of these rules are centuries old, but most were formulated in the decades that followed the Second World War, during a time when the corporate world was flooded with management strategies that promised a more effective workplace. Yet while these strategies explained how to start up, lead or restructure a company, and how to optimise processes and motivate your employees, they didn't explain what those things are actually *like*.

That is the realm of unwritten rules. They have become a sort of anthology of working life; not a prophet so much as a good friend. Over the years, these little pearls of wisdom have circulated in open-plan offices, been photocopied, passed around, rewritten, expanded on – and often also forgotten.

In this book, we've brought together what we think are the most useful rules for work, relationships and other challenges. Some are a little tongue-in-cheek, others emit a sort of Zen-like wisdom – but they all have two things in common. First, they're short; second, they're more than mere observations: they help us make sense of and navigate the absurdities of everyday life. They also always have these three important questions in their sights:

Have I interpreted this situation, person or problem correctly?

What's the best course of action here?

Am I on the right track?

If you have headspace, time and good advice at your disposal, you will always find an answer. But if you find yourself in an uncertain and fast-moving situation, or if you just want a quick overview and need to make an on-the-spot decision – that's when these rules come into their own, because they help you focus on what is important.

Of course, not every problem can be resolved via a split-second decision. Also, what works for one person won't necessarily work for everyone – so don't blindly follow every rule in this book; instead, consider each of them carefully to work out if a rule fits with your way of working, your situation and your goal.

By the way, we should point out that these rules did not originate with us. We have merely collected, explained, categorised and visualised them (and, we hope, not misunderstood them). So anything clever you find in this book isn't our idea but someone else's. And there's a rule about that too: *If you think that you have a new idea, you are wrong. Someone probably already had it* (Sutton's law, p. 70).

Part 1. How to Survive Meetings, Deadlines and Other Workplace Adventures

THE KETCHUP EFFECT: FIRST NOTHING ... THEN EVERYTHING ALL AT ONCE

Ketchup refusing to come out of the bottle is perhaps the best metaphor for life generally. (We're talking here about glass bottles, not those soulless plastic ones that allow you to cheat by squeezing them.) This is how it usually happens: you open the bottle and tilt it at a 45-degree angle. You wait. You tilt it at a 90-degree angle. And wait. Then you lose patience and start slapping the bottom of the bottle. Then you shake it. But still ... nothing. And then, suddenly, here it comes, but not the dollop you were after, no, your burger almost drowns in a flood of the stuff.

This phenomenon has a name: it's the ketchup effect.

Nothing happens for a long time, and then everything happens all at once.

You'll encounter it everywhere in life. You're waiting for a bus, and then three come along at once. A friend spends years looking for an affordable place to rent, then suddenly has four options and can't decide which to go for. Or take the freelancer who says yes to every project out of fear that work will dry up – only to find herself swamped when everything is due on the same day.

The ketchup effect: Nothing ... nothing ... nothing ... everything all at once.

But there is also a more positive side to the ketchup effect, often associated with times when the tide suddenly turns in your favour: for example, the moment you discover you're no longer on your own and that other people welcome – rather than ridicule or oppose – your ideas. It's the moment when what once felt frustrating suddenly seems easy (keep in mind the risk of the situation getting out of control and the entire bottle of ketchup splashing out).

What can trigger a ketchup effect?

You might think it's whoever is brave enough to take the first step and propose something new. Yes, that person is important; to stick with the ketchup metaphor, they are the one who opens the bottle, but do they create the actual effect? No. In a brilliant TED Talk from 2010, Derek Sivers observed that the first person who says yes to your proposal is key. Once one person agrees (the 'first follower'), maybe another joins in, and soon a constellation of lone fighters has transformed into a group. And then the tipping point comes, i.e. the ketchup starts flowing.

We frequently underestimate the importance of these 'first followers'. Let's look at an example: Emmeline Pankhurst was the founder of the suffragette movement in the UK. Everyone knows her name – she was the one who unscrewed the cap. But how many of her supporters can you name? They included her daughters, with whose help she brought in other like-minded women until a proper movement emerged, which put more and more pressure on the government – until it was finally forced to give in and grant women the vote.

The ketchup effect serves as a reminder that it isn't all about the leader. The followers matter too. Without them, there would – by definition – be no leader. So, if you find yourself in a situation where someone's ketchup refuses to come out of the bottle, ask yourself whether you could be the one to turn the tide by saying yes.

STURGEON'S LAW: WHY NINETY PER CENT OF EVERYTHING IS RUBBISH

At a reading at New York University – so the story goes – novelist and short-story writer Theodore Sturgeon (1918–1985) vented his frustration at the fact that science fiction was the only literary genre people judged by its worst examples, rather than its best:

'You say "Ninety per cent of science fiction is crap." Well, you're right. Ninety per cent of sci-fi is crap. But ninety per cent of *everything* is crap. Everything – cars, books, cheese, haircuts, people – is crap, except for the ten per cent that we happen to like.'

This has since become known as Sturgeon's law:

Ninety per cent of everything is rubbish.

Sturgeon was obviously exaggerating, but we can surely all agree with the point he was making: most things *are* crap. Most meetings we attend, most things we buy, most of the stuff we see on Instagram (and certainly the things we, the authors of this book, post) are rubbish. Even most of our hopes and fears are rubbish.

But careful: don't get too comfortable with this idea, because if ninety per cent of everything is rubbish, that includes the observation that 'ninety per cent of everything is rubbish'. Right? What Sturgeon was doing was criticising the critics. It's easy to find mistakes and to know better. Anyone can say 'Ninety per cent of what management is doing is crap.' But according to Sturgeon, ninety per cent of our opinions are also crap.

The rule is useful in two ways. For us as consumers, it acts as a reminder not to believe everything someone says, writes or promises. It's worth taking a closer look, asking questions, thinking for yourself. Conversely, it is also a good idea to be a little generous about ninety per cent of things that are said, written or done: people don't usually mean to perform badly, it's just that not everything can be in that top 10 per cent. Meanwhile, for creators, it is a reminder that only a few things are properly excellent, and we need to produce, test and discard a lot of stuff in order to occasionally achieve something first-rate.

Sturgeon's law is thus a kind of control mechanism. Is what I'm doing here right now relevant, meaningful or *really* good? If not, is it at least good enough? If not, then start over again.

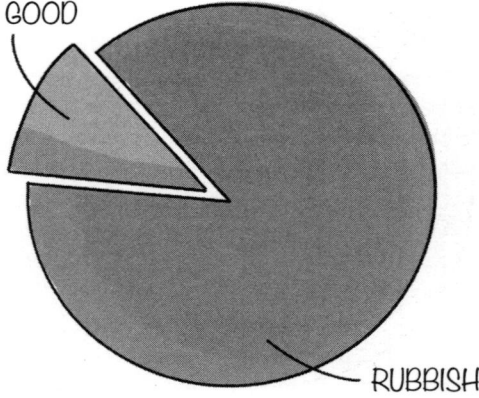

Sturgeon's Law: Ninety per cent of everything is rubbish.

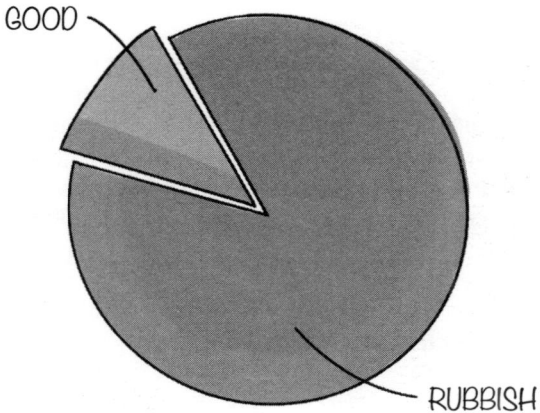

PARKINSON'S LAW: WHY THERE'S SO LITTLE TIME (AND SO MUCH TO DO)

The modern workplace is complex, and so are our jobs. There's too much to do, and too little time in which to do it. Entire fields of research, stacks of self-help books and the careers of countless life coaches have been devoted to this topic. One of the most clear-sighted statements on the topic was formulated by British historian C. Northcote Parkinson in 1955:

Work expands so as to fill the time available for its completion (rather than according to its complexity).

What does that mean? It means that if you schedule two hours for a meeting, it'll take at least two hours; if you schedule fifteen minutes, it'll take at least fifteen minutes. If you have three months to hand in a piece of coursework, you'll hand it in on the very last day (if at all); if you have half an hour, you'll do it in half an hour (if at all).

This realisation may be less weighty than Newton's gravitational constant, but it is just as accurate: the fact that a meeting, project or any other task takes at least as much time as you've allowed for it, and not a second less, seems to be a law of nature. Parkinson's law may have been intended as a humorous comment on the increasing bureaucratisation of life, but to us it reveals a simple truth about the modern world. After all, hasn't every procrastinator in the world (us included) experienced this phenomenon first hand? The most well-disciplined working group will complete most of its task just in the nick of time, and, even in the most agile organisation, meetings last *at least* as long as scheduled.

Here's an idea for how to use rule to your advantage:

When you embark on a new project, set yourself two intermediate deadlines in addition to the real deadline – and then 'complete' the project (the task, the piece of writing, whatever it might be) three times in total, aiming to improve the end product each time. Be ruthless in your execution: as you finish each version, make sure that it really is finished, so that, if you had to, you could submit, publish or go live with it right there and then.

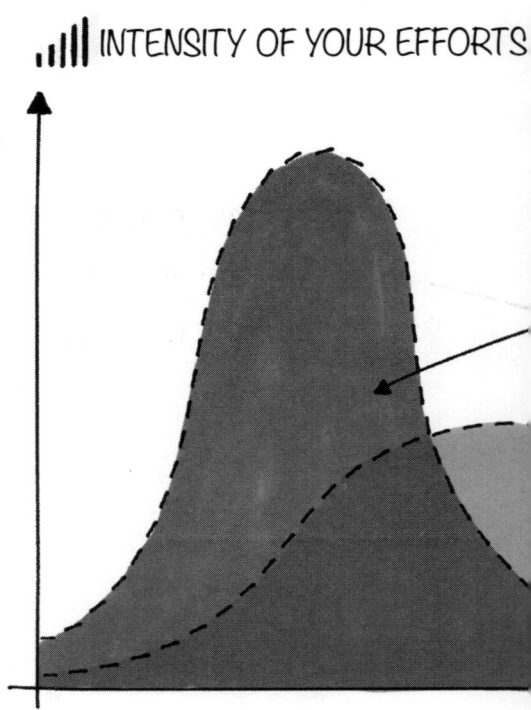

Work expands to fill the time available for it.

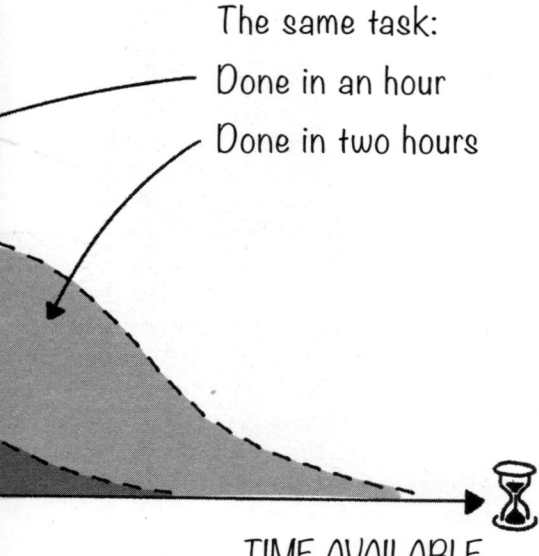

THE 333 METHOD: WHAT A PERFECT WORKING DAY LOOKS LIKE

What would your working day have to look like, for you not to get the Sunday blues? Oliver Burkeman, author of the bestselling *Four Thousand Weeks*, argues that to rediscover the joy of work we should do less – but do it properly. To help us do that, he suggests using the 333 method.

Now, we know what you're thinking: the 80/20 rule, the 10-10-10 method, the 08/15 rule ... All those formulas are getting a bit tiresome, aren't they? Without wanting to overstate our importance, we, as authors, are in part to blame for that. And with a bit of tweaking, the 333 rule is one that we've found truly helpful when it comes to regaining a modicum of control over our working days:

Identify your most important current project, and work on it for **three** hours. Spend that time working only on that project. Ideally, do it in the morning, when your brain is still fresh. Complete **three** maintenance tasks that need doing if you want to stay on top of things at work (e.g. deal with emails, take meetings, solve problems). Do **three** personal care tasks to keep things running smoothly in your private life (e.g. work on your relationship, do some exercise, household chores).

Three hours of deep work, three maintenance tasks, three personal care tasks.

HOFSTADTER'S LAW: THINGS ALWAYS TAKE LONGER THAN EXPECTED

Researchers at the University of Waterloo in Canada once asked students to predict how long it would take them to write their final thesis. The respondents on average estimated 34 days: a little over a month. The researchers then asked them to estimate how long it would take if everything went smoothly (27 days), and the absolute worst case scenario (48 days). How long do you think it actually took the students to write their theses?

Longer?

Correct. Much longer.

To be precise, it took 55.5 days on average. Which is a whole week (15 per cent) longer than the supposed worst case scenario, and three weeks (or 60 per cent) longer than the most likely one.

History is full of incorrect estimates. When construction on Berlin's new airport started in 2006, the engineers, construction planners and architects calculated that it would be completed by 2011. The airport eventually opened its gates in autumn 2020, nine years after the projected completion date. Compared with that, the Canadian students

Time is relatively long.

who handed in their dissertations a mere three weeks late look like overachievers.

In 1979, computer scientist and author Douglas Hofstadter turned the widespread problem of everything taking longer than anticipated into a kind of reflexive statement, which he called Hofstadter's law:

It always takes longer than you expect, even when you take into account Hofstadter's law.

Even when we know that things always take longer than planned, we still fall into the same old trap and are convinced that this time it will be different. There is also an extended version of Hofstadter's law:

It always takes longer than you expect, even when you take into account Hofstadter's law ... and in the end it will also cost twice as much and be only half as good as you'd hoped.

This is how to deal with Hofstadter's law:

1. **Don't trust your judgement.**
   When you plan a project, be sceptical about your own sense of time, and ask someone external who has done similar projects to estimate how long it will take. Then add at least 15 per cent – ideally 60 per cent.

2. **Define the path as well as the goal.**
   A study once asked participants to gauge how long it would take them to complete a piece of writing; and additionally asked half the group to specify where and when they would be working on it. The result was that the participants who were asked to define their

process both came up with more realistic deadlines and completed the task faster. So don't just specify when you'll be done – specify when you'll be working on it too.

3. Don't worry if it still takes you longer.

Because it always takes longer than you expect, even when you take into account Hofstadter's law.

PLOTZ'S LAW: ASK YOURSELF THIS QUESTION BEFORE YOU SAY YES

In a 2014 column for *Slate*, journalist David Plotz came up with a quick rule for how to make decisions. We're calling it Plotz's law – though to be fair, he says in the article that 'to give credit where it's due, this titbit was passed along to me by my wife, Hanna Rosin, and her friend, *New Yorker* staff writer Margaret Talbot, so it could also be called the Rosin–Talbot law. Plotz started with the following anecdote, which we've adapted slightly.

Assume you're invited to give a talk in six months' time. You're surprised, and flattered too, and you'll even be paid a pretty decent fee.

So you're happy – even though deep down you're slightly nervous about it, because you don't enjoy public speaking. Also, isn't the audience at that event known for being extremely demanding and don't they usually only invite top-notch speakers? You're a little unsure whether it's such a good idea after all. Luckily, there's still a while to go. A whole six months! And you'll definitely find the right topic for the occasion, even for an audience as picky as this one. No need to worry, then, there's plenty of time. So you say yes.

Plotz's law: Would I do it tomorrow?

And that's a mistake. Because here is what's going to happen: even if, right now, the talk seems far away, at some point it won't be so far away anymore. It's not as if you've been procrastinating: you have been thinking about the event a lot, while also telling yourself that you still have ages to go – but suddenly it's only days away, and you've got nothing. And right now, all sorts of things are going on in your life, and you're feeling the pressure. That subconscious nervous feeling you already had six months ago is now very much a conscious dread.

In Plotz's words, 'The opportunity that sparkled so brightly when they flattered you into it six months ago isn't gleaming anymore. It's just a gigantic hassle.'

We've all been there. We've all said yes to something we know we don't have the ability, time or energy to do – or, well, simply don't feel like doing. But because that something is ages away, we assume that by then we'll have the ability, time, energy and inclination to do it.

The most important question to ask yourself before you agree to do anything is this:

Would I do it tomorrow?

Not 'Would I do it at some hypothetical point in the future?' but 'Would I reschedule the things I planned to do tomorrow to do this thing instead?'

This five-word rule doesn't tell us to say no to everything that could prove a challenge; otherwise we would soon stop doing anything altogether. What it does suggest is that you don't say yes to something on the assumption that you'll have more time to do it when the day eventually comes around. You're unlikely to have more time in future. If you wouldn't do it tomorrow, don't agree to do it in six months' time.

THE PARETO PRINCIPLE: SOMETIMES LESS IS MORE

Once upon a time (in the late nineteenth century), a man was working in his garden when he suddenly noticed that not every pea plant had the same number of pods. He harvested the peas and sorted them according to their parent plants, then did some calculations – and realised that just 20 per cent of plants supplied 80 per cent of the peas.

It may be just an anecdote, but what we know for sure is that our man in the garden, Vilfredo Pareto (1848–1923), didn't stop at peas. He was an economics professor at the University of Lausanne, and he decided to apply his discovery apropos peas to an entirely different field: wealth distribution. From this, he subsequently realised that in his home country, Italy, around 80 per cent of land belonged to 20 per cent of the population – the same distribution as for his peas. In 1906, he wrote about it in his seminal work *Manuale di economia politica* (*Manual of Political Economy*).

However, it was the management consultant Joseph Juran who, in the 1940s, applied this observation to the business world, and transformed the idea that a small number of inputs creates the majority of outcomes into the so-called Pareto principle.

80 per cent of output is generated by 20 per cent of input.

This is also known as the 80/20 rule:

80 per cent of output is generated by 20 per cent of input.

Of course, it's not always *exactly* true. The 80/20 rule does not mean that the ratio is always precisely 80:20. It also tends to be *felt* rather than measured or scientifically proven. But if you open your eyes, you can see – or rather feel – it everywhere: 20 per cent of decisions lead to 80 per cent of results (we wrote about this in *The Decision Book*); 20 per cent of customers (or products) produce 80 per cent of turnover; 20 per cent of tasks cause 80 per cent of stress. But it is also true that the last 20 per cent of a project requires as much effort (and time) as the first 80 per cent.

Let's look at this last example: difficult as it may be to accept, finishing something is at least as laborious as being *nearly* finished with it. So always schedule more time (see Hofstadter's law).

We might also take a different approach: we could decide to be satisfied with 80 per cent. Sure, no one wants 80 per cent of a house or 80 per cent of a kidney transplant, but when it comes to everyday tasks and projects – a design, thesis or presentation, say – sometimes 80 per cent is good enough. We often turn into perfectionists when we reach the home straight, getting tangled up in details that consume endless time and resources without really making things any better.

Instead, we could try being happy with a less than perfect outcome. The difficulty lies in knowing when something *has* to be perfect, and when good enough is good enough – which is harder than it sounds.

It's well worth applying the Pareto principle to your own life, and asking yourself, objectively, what 80/20 situations you can spot there. Author James Clear calls it 'living the Pareto principle lifestyle', and it's best done on a cold, grey Sunday afternoon, sitting on the sofa wrapped in a blanket. Take a moment, maybe pick up your diary, review the last twelve months, and ask yourself:

Job. What did I do that had the most impact?

Friendship. Which encounters enriched my life most?

Soul. Which situations upset and stressed me out most?

Or why not come up with your own categories and questions, and take a little time to find out – as Vilfredo Pareto did 130 years ago – which 'pea plants' in your 'garden' are bearing the most peas.

PARKINSON'S LAW OF TRIVIALITY: WHY EVERYONE HAS AN OPINION

Picture this: you're attending a finance committee meeting with ten other people. There are three topics on the agenda:

- A proposal for a nuclear reactor costing £10m
- A proposal for a bike shed costing £350
- A proposal for an annual coffee budget of £21.

What an odd meeting, you think. Aren't those budgets a bit ... well, unexpectedly low? We were stumped too at first, but it turns out to be an example used in 1957 by British historian C. Northcote Parkinson (the same man who gave us the other Parkinson's law that we looked at earlier) to illustrate triviality.

So, what happens next at this fictional meeting?

You start discussing the reactor. It quickly becomes clear that seven of the eleven participants know less than nothing about nuclear reactors – and, of the remaining four, only two know how much they cost. One of these two people makes an informed suggestion, which the committee, in its ignorance, rejects. Another wonders if they should explain

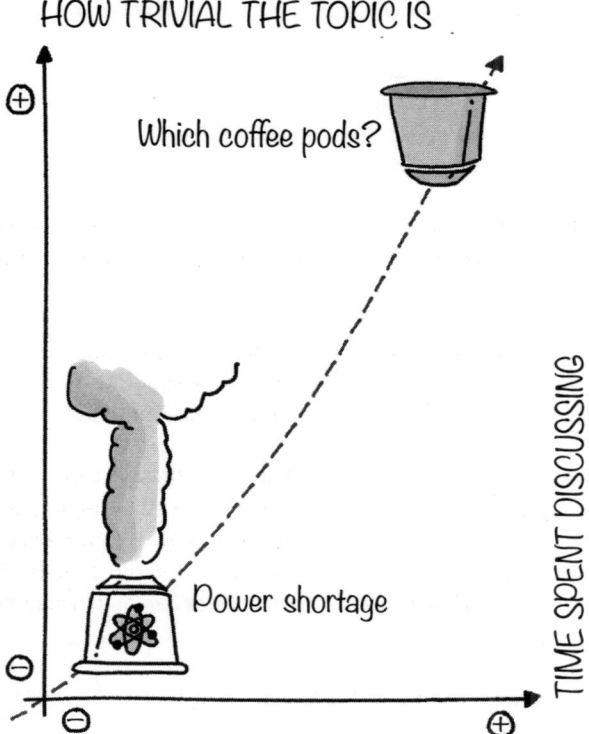

The more trivial the topic, the more intense the debate.

to the rest of the group how reactors work, but suspects that no one will have the foggiest what to do with that information, and so decides to say nothing.

A few minutes later, the committee turns to the next item on the agenda: building a new bike shed for £350. The debate is instantly in full swing, because everyone knows what a bike shed is. You all argue heatedly about whether the roof should be aluminium, asbestos or galvanised iron. You spend three quarters of an hour on this, and finally settle on a design that will save about £50. You lean back in your chairs in the satisfaction of knowing that you've come to an important decision.

Then the committee tackles the final item: the coffee budget. Now everyone's truly in their element. Even non-coffee-drinkers add their tuppence worth. You spend more time talking about coffee than about the bike shed and the reactor combined. In the end, you run out of time and schedule a further meeting to resolve the issue.

Parkinson called this the law of triviality:

The time spent on any item of the agenda will be in inverse proportion to the sum involved.

The smaller the issue, the longer the debate – it's a phenomenon that reflects our tendency to focus on banalities and avoid more complex matters. We call such time-wasting discussions 'bike shedding', as in 'We've bike-shedded it.'

We bike-shed because talking about simple things is easy, whereas it's harder to tackle the complicated, weightier issues – even if they are more important. Here's a little trick: next time you're holding an agenda in your hand, jot down next to each item how much time to allocate to it in the meeting. The easy ones get a narrow slot, the trickier subjects a bigger one.

BROOKS' LAW: DO WE NEED A BIGGER TEAM?

Fred Brooks (1931–2022), brain-in-chief at IBM, was the boss of thousands of programmers in his day. So he knew his way around computers – and around people. He noticed something interesting: when you give a team that's having trouble meeting a deadline more manpower to help it catch up, what often happens is the opposite. Instead of working faster, the team slows down. Interestingly, the new members are slowing down the old. He turned this into the eponymous Brooks' law:

Adding manpower to a late project makes it later.

Brooks was no fool. He knew full well that such a simplistic claim relating to team dynamics couldn't possibly be universally true. Yet the law became famous among management teams everywhere during the 1970s and 80s, so clearly people thought that there was (and we think still *is*) something to it. Many felt they could recognise themselves in his observation: that adding new people *does* often have a detrimental impact on a team. We can only guess the reason: perhaps the new team members think they know better, which irritates rather than motivates the existing team. Or perhaps they don't understand how things work yet, and take too long to get up to speed. Or perhaps it's simply the age-old case of too many cooks spoiling the broth.

The problem with expanding teams most likely has to do with communication. The numbers prove it: in a team of five, there are ten communication pathways (see the illustration). If you add two more people, there are suddenly twenty-one pathways.

At some point, someone expanded on Brooks' law to describe an efficiency strategy referred to as a Bermuda plan:

Tell most of the staff to take a holiday, and let the best guys take care of the rest of the work.

Brooks' law and its Bermuda 'extension' don't provide a blueprint for cutting costs, but they do centre on a pair of interesting questions that anyone in charge of a project should ask themselves (when they have a spare moment):

1. **The Bermuda question.** Who in my team can I truly trust? Who, if need be, will get stuck in and get us out of a mess?
2. **The Brooks question.** If I could add three new people to the team, who would they be? And how would that change the team's dynamic?

OUR TEAM (5)...

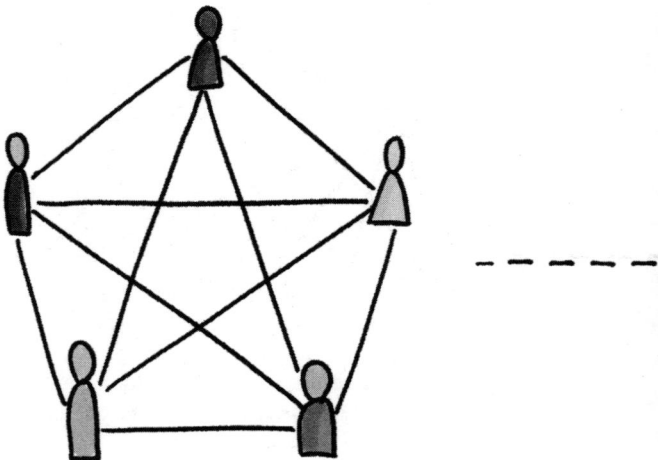

Brooks' law: Adding manpower to a late project makes it later.

...IS EXPANDED (7)

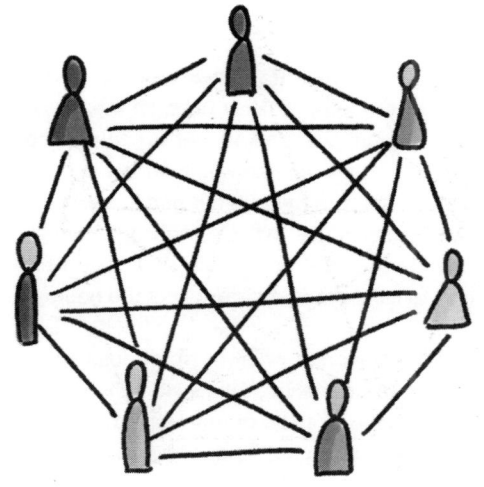

GOODHART'S LAW: METRICS ARE NOT THE SAME AS GOALS

During the British Raj, there was a cobra plague in Delhi. The government took an unusual measure: it announced that it would pay a bounty for every dead cobra. At first, it looked like the scheme would succeed, because there was a sharp spike in the number of dead cobras dropped off at the bounty office. As it turned out, though, enterprising members of the population had begun breeding cobras *only* to kill them and then collect the bounty.

The phenomenon whereby an attempt to solve a problem only ends up making things worse is known as the cobra effect (a.k.a. the law of unintended consequences, which we will discuss later). The term was coined by the German economist Horst Siebert (1938–2009) in a book by the same title.

Let's apply this to the workplace: the number of dead cobras was the metric to be achieved, and the bounty was the incentive. Nowadays, every company has its metrics: it might be the number of cars sold a month, customers gained per ad campaign, or, as in the illustration, how much tomato soup is produced. You'll find metrics at school too (known as 'grades'), and every kind of sport has metrics that athletes are incentivised to exceed; metrics allow us to be measured and compared.

But metrics are not the same as goals. And the problem is that to achieve them you sometimes do things that take you further from the goal. You may, for instance, breed cobras, and then kill them to prove that you've killed a large number of cobras. The government gets its metric, but it doesn't achieve its goal. Some among you will be reminded of your own jobs, where you're constantly chasing metrics while getting ever further away from your real goal. This process can be described thus:

If a measure becomes a target, it ceases to be a good measure.

This idea is now popularly known as Goodhart's law, after the British economist Charles Goodhart, who originally used it to critique Margaret Thatcher's economic policies.

When the metric becomes the goal, we often strive to achieve it at any cost, without realising that we might end up missing – or worse, endangering – the real goal.

If a measure becomes a target, it becomes a bad measure.

THE LOCKSMITH'S PARADOX: WHY IDEAS ARE EXPENSIVE

One day, Pablo Picasso was strolling through a market when a woman stopped him in his tracks.

'I'm a big fan of your art, Mr Picasso!' she said. 'Would you mind sketching a little something on this piece of paper for me?'

Picasso smiled, took the piece of paper and drew a cute little flower. When he was done, he said, 'That'll be a million francs.'

'Good God!' replied the woman. 'It took you no more than thirty seconds to draw it, how can it cost that much?'

Picasso replied, 'My dear lady, it took thirty years for me to be able to draw that in thirty seconds.'

This oft-told story probably never happened, but it's fun; and it nicely illustrates a fascinating phenomenon called the 'locksmith's paradox', which deals with the effort–value ratio:

The longer it takes, the more we value it.

The longer something takes to do, the more we value it.

And we do this because we don't realise how much effort it takes to be able to do something quickly.

The term 'locksmith's paradox' was coined by Dan Ariely, professor of psychology and behavioural economics at Duke University in North Carolina.

Back in 2010, he met a locksmith who told him that when he was an apprentice it often took him a long time to fix a lock; he often broke the lock in the process and had to charge the customer for a replacement. But still, his customers paid without complaining and frequently even gave him a tip, so grateful were they that he had fixed their problem.

Over time, he got better at his job; soon, he was able to change a lock much faster, in less than a minute, and didn't break it. But then his customers started complaining about being overcharged. The outcome was the same – he fixed their problem – but what had changed was their perception of the value, of the effort involved. Why did it cost so much, they wondered, when it had only taken him a moment?

The locksmith's paradox is a classic problem in the creative industries. Sometimes a great idea comes to you in less than a minute, sometimes it takes three weeks. Is it worth more or less because of that? A hairdresser can give someone the same haircut over and over again, but an idea isn't something that you can force or mass-produce – so how do you work out what it's worth?

According to Ariely, our valuation of goods and services is based not only on their usefulness, but also on our sense of what is fair, given the effort that goes into them. But we forget that there is also an unseen effort, such as years of training – or, as the case may be, a flash of inspiration, which may appear instantly or take three weeks to show up.

MURPHY'S LAW: (NOT) EVERYTHING THAT CAN GO WRONG WILL GO WRONG

The projector fails at the exact moment you're about to start a hugely important client presentation. You're on your way to a first date, suddenly the train brakes and you spill coffee all over your lap. You've just switched lanes in heavy traffic, only for your old lane to start moving faster, while the new one grinds to a halt. As Murphy's law (a.k.a. Sod's law) says:

If something can go wrong, it will.

It is the pessimists' motto and the fatalists' favourite saying, and the ultimate answer to the eternal question, 'Why does it always happen to me?'

In reality, of course, we know that not everything that can go wrong *does* go wrong – nor does it *always* happen to this or that person. The fact is, we only recall the times when things went pear-shaped better than the times when, say, we managed *not* to get coffee on our trousers.

'Toast always falls buttered side down' is perhaps the best-known example of Murphy's law. But is it true? In his article 'Tumbling toast, Murphy's law and the fundamental constants', mathematician Robert Matthews worked out that

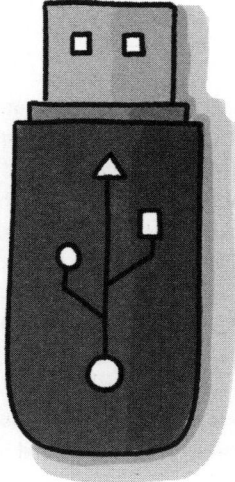

No matter which way up you insert your USB stick, it's never the right way.

it's a matter of physics, rather than bad luck: the distance between the plate on the table and the floor on which it lands is only long enough for your slice of toast to go through half a rotation – and because we (usually) put it on the plate buttered side up, it will inevitably land face down. To avoid that happening, we either need to start using taller tables, or put our toast on the plate face down.

Who discovered Murphy's law?

In the late 1940s, the US Air Force conducted a series of experiments in the Mojave Desert to test the effects of extreme acceleration and deceleration on the human body. Medical officer John Paul Stapp would strap himself to a rocket-powered sled that ran on tracks and launch himself at high speeds through the desert before braking sharply. To measure the pressures he was exposed to in the process, an engineer called Edward Murphy developed a special sensor, but his technicians mounted it on the rocket sled incorrectly – whereupon Murphy drily remarked something like, 'If there's a way to do it wrong, those guys will find it.' Afterwards, when Colonel Stapp described the daring experiment at a press conference, one journalist asked why no one was injured. Stapp proudly explained that they'd taken 'Murphy's law' into account, which allowed them to put in place all necessary safeguards.

Hang on. Wait. What?

As it turns out, all this time we've entirely misunderstood Murphy's law. Far from expressing the fatalistic view that everything is doomed from the start, they were instead the words of someone striving for engineering excellence. This, at least, is what Nick Spark argues in his book *A History of*

Murphy's Law. According to Sparks, what the law states is that if you work out all the things that can possibly go wrong in advance, you can reduce the likelihood of disaster striking. Who knew?

Part 2. When You're Convinced You Should Be Doing Everything Differently

CHESTERTON'S FENCE: TO CHANGE OR NOT TO CHANGE

A pedestrian notices a fence being put up across a street. At first, he can't tell what it's for. On closer inspection, its purpose is still unclear. He says to the workers, 'Pull it down.' To which one of them replies, 'If you don't see the point of the fence, I won't let you get rid of it. Go away and think about it a little, and if after that you come back and tell me that you now understand its purpose, then maybe I'll let you tear it down.'

This parable from 1929 is nicknamed 'Chesterton's fence'. First published in an essay collection by G. K. Chesterton (1874–1936), it is meant as a cautionary tale: don't change something – processes, systems, whatever it might be – if you don't know why it was introduced in the first place.

Here's an example from the business world that you might be familiar with from your own organisation. A new manager has come in, and is seeking ways to reduce costs while trying to look like they are up on the latest trends. They decide to turn HQ into an open-plan office, for two reasons: to increase communication between employees by removing walls and opening doors, and to reduce overheads by fitting more people into the space. But we know the damage such a move can cause: open-plan offices lead to more sick days (because germs spread more easily), make it harder for people to focus and – unexpectedly, perhaps, and for various reasons – decrease, rather than increase, face-to-face interaction between staff.

Going back to Chesterton's parable, we can say that the new manager hasn't taken into account the reason the fence (in this case, walls and doors) was put up in the first place. The manager has introduced a change without considering the possible consequences; and the best way to predict such consequences of a change is to ask *why* the status quo is what it is. In the case of offices, doors and walls screen out noise and create privacy, which allows staff to concentrate better and promotes well-being.

Don't change something before you understand why it was done in the first place.

There are plenty more examples from the real world to support Chesterton's notion. The privatisation boom of the 1990s, for instance, and the gradual dismantling of social welfare, were driven by the desire for short-term gains – and we have learnt the painful way that they in fact served a crucial function. This doesn't mean that you should never change anything. Chesterton's fence is often used to justify a reactionary attitude, but it doesn't suggest that everything should always stay the same. Rather, that you should find out why the thing you want to change exists. We can safely assume that nobody is going round putting up fences all over the place from sheer boredom. If you take the time to discover the reason for the fence, and after careful consideration decide that it is no longer useful, then by all means go and tear it down.

Chesterton's fence: Don't change something before you understand why it was done in the first place.

AMARA'S LAW: WHY WE MISJUDGE THE IMPACT OF NEW THINGS

In the 1960s, systems engineer Roy Amara realised that our attitude to technological innovation is paradoxical: we welcome it, but often have unrealistic expectations – that is, we quickly get excited about something new, but are just as quickly disappointed if it doesn't work as well as we expect. According to Amara:

We tend to overestimate the impact of new things, before underestimating them later.

Innovation always encounters some resistance, of course. Humans tend to like continuity and fear change. According to Amara, we are particularly bad with new technology: we expect too much from it too quickly, and don't fully understand that anything new needs time to develop. A lot of time.

Take AI: our initial reaction to it was a mix of euphoria and pessimism. Some people knelt before it as if before an apparition of the Virgin Mary, others danced the apocalypso. Since then, we have gained more perspective, and our enthusiasm as well as our fears have diminished somewhat.

You can apply Amara's law to lots of different scenarios. For instance, whenever we make a change designed to improve some aspect of our well-being – take up meditation, try a new workout, go on the keto diet – we're inclined to get very excited about it very quickly, overestimating its ability to fix us. And then, when it doesn't meet our expectations straight away, we chuck the whole thing in. The point is this: most of us don't stick with things long enough to discover just how useful they really are.

Or take relationships: you meet someone. you like them, you fall in love. You see them through rose-tinted glasses. And then you start noticing the flaws; the things you used to find adorable are now just annoying. But if you stay the course – even after you've realised that the person you love isn't perfect (and neither are you) – the tide may turn. If you can learn to love yourself and the other person despite your respective imperfections, you will grow even closer.

In short, Amara's law doesn't apply only to technology:

When it comes to people too, we tend to overestimate in the short run and underestimate in the long run.

TODAY

Amara's law: We tend to overestimate the impact of a new technology, before going on to underestimate it later.

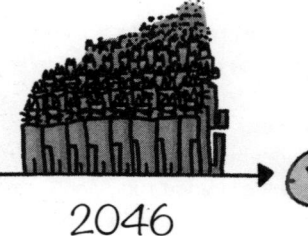

2046

THE KISS PRINCIPLE:
SIMPLIFY, SIMPLIFY, SIMPLIFY

During the Second World War, Clarence 'Kelly' Johnson, an aviation engineer at Lockheed, tasked his team with creating a jet engine that could be repaired by an average mechanic in battle conditions with just a few tools. His motto for the project was:

KISS – Keep it simple stupid.

In other words: 'Build an engine that's so "simple and stupid" that you don't need sophisticated tools to repair it.'

Who knows whether the legend is true – Johnson's usual motto seems to have been 'Be quick, be quiet, be on time' (also quite a good rule, don't you think?) – but KISS has since become a guiding principle for designers, coders, copywriters and product developers everywhere seeking simplicity in their creations.

Everyone likes clarity and simplicity, but we're all prone to using overblown jargon on occasion; we all want a simple fix and yet we're often more convinced by a flashy presentation than a straightforward idea. Even as we keep insisting on streamlining our lives, the world around us is becoming ever more elaborate: new products, add-ons and updates continue to crop up everywhere – and while most of them have to some extent made life easier, many have made it more complicated and exhausting. Speaking of jargon, this balancing act between our happiness and the growing complexity of everyday life is called 'simplexity'.

Meanwhile, 'simple' shouldn't be confused with 'easy'. Streamlining requires a hefty dose of understanding, dedication and time. 'Keep it simple stupid' can be interpreted as an act of resistance against the too-muchness of things, against the notion that more is always better and complicated equals smarter. If we force ourselves to simplify, we can fight jargon and over-stimulation.

However, KISS doesn't mean renouncing complexity, ambiguity and multi-layeredness wholesale – it merely asks that we be precise, accessible and clear.

KISS: Keep it simple stupid.

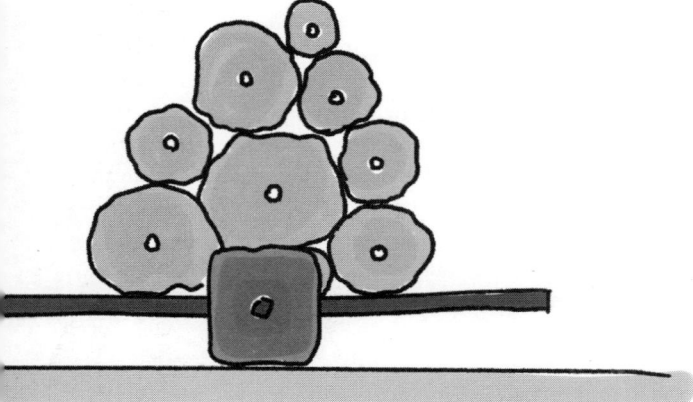

SUTTON'S LAW: STANDING ON THE SHOULDERS OF GIANTS

Sutton's law makes an important statement about creativity:

If you think that you have a new idea, you are wrong. Someone probably already had it.

History is full of supposedly ground-breaking ideas that were in fact nothing new – merely borrowed, adapted or transformed. Pythagoras' theorem was already known to ancient Babylonians and Indians long before he was born. The iPhone was not the first smartphone – only the first to combine a touch screen, browser and app store. And Shakespeare's *Romeo and Juliet* was inspired by Ovid's tale of Pyramus and Thisbe.

We know that new ideas don't emerge in a vacuum. Which means that they're never the final version: they are continuously being critiqued, updated and improved upon. Which in turn means that they don't belong to anyone. Innovation, then, is not about creating something from nothing, but about finding new and better ways to use something that already exists. What matters is not who had the idea first, but how it is best taken forward.

The law we quoted at the start of this chapter obviously isn't one we've come up with ourselves. We got it from organisational psychologist Robert Sutton. The full version goes like this:

If you think that you have a new idea, you are wrong. Someone probably already had it. This idea isn't original either; I stole it from someone else.

Let's look at another example. There is actually *another* Sutton's law, which is very similar to Occam's razor, proving that Sutton's observation is a self-fulfilling prophesy: that there really are no new ideas under the sun.

So, whenever you have an inkling that you might have stumbled on an 'original' idea, don't be protective: be generous and curious, and glad when someone else uses it, develops it further – or even disproves it.

Sutton's law: If you think that you have a new idea, you are wrong. Someone probably already had it.

No, I'm the original!

Errr... guys...

20 000 BCE

STRUMMER'S LAW: NOTHING COMES FROM NOTHING

Joe Strummer, lead singer of the Clash, once said:

No input, no output.

In a way, it's a trivial statement. Even a toddler knows that you have to fill a glass with water before drinking it. But it still provides food for thought: you cannot create something by yourself. To produce any output, you need input from others, who in turn will have taken on output from someone else.

But we shouldn't confuse mindlessly scrolling through social media with input. Liking lots of posts is not the same as delving properly into a specific piece of content. Nothing against social media, but input is work, scrolling is distraction. Input means engaging with something – whether a book, a thought, a person ... or an online post.

Good input = good output.

THE CANADA PRINCIPLE: BEWARE LOW-HANGING FRUIT

Netflix started off as a mail-order DVD rental business. According to its co-founder Marc Randolph, once it went big in the US, expanding into the Canadian market seemed a no-brainer. 'It was close, the regulations were easy and transport costs were low. When we ran the numbers, we saw that we could probably get an instant revenue bump of about 10 per cent,' he recalls. Canada was low-hanging fruit, a way to achieve maximum gain with minimal effort. Yet they decided against sending DVDs to Canada. Why?

Randolph's reasoning was this. Although in the short term Netflix could make money from extending its business to Canada, complications such as the different currencies and the language barrier (in the French-speaking provinces) would stymie the business in the long term. Randolph turned this into a rule that he called the Canada principle: *What looks like low-hanging fruit usually isn't low-hanging fruit.*

Don't blindly chase after every tempting opportunity. Check carefully whether it will be useful in the long run or will just distract you from your goal. What looks like a great opportunity usually requires more work and effort than you think. Nothing happens just like that. Everything takes time and thought. Time and attentiveness are your most valuable resources. Handle them with care.

THE LAW OF UNINTENDED CONSEQUENCES: WHY THINGS NEVER TURN OUT AS YOU EXPECT

In 1936, sociologist Robert Merton came up with the 'law of unintended consequences': when an act designed to achieve something, e.g. fix a problem, ends up doing something completely different. This happens in one of three ways:

1. The problem isn't fixed, but something good comes of it. When the Tower of Pisa was built, it was of course supposed to be vertical, but the unstable subsoil caused one side of the tower to start sinking – inadvertently turning it into a tourist attraction. *The plan failed, but it had a positive outcome.*

2. The problem is fixed, but there are side effects. US prohibition (1920–33) significantly reduced the consumption of alcohol, but also caused a sharp rise in alcohol-associated crime. *The plan failed because it succeeded.*

3. The problem isn't fixed, and what happens is the opposite of what you expected. In 2003, a photographer published thousands of aerial shots he had taken to document erosion and development along California's coastline. One of the photos happened to be of Barbra Streisand's house, and Streisand sued him for invasion of privacy. Yet all the lawsuit did was to draw everyone's attention to the photo's existence, with hundreds of thousands of viewers visiting the website to take a good look at Streisand's house. *Streisand's plan failed because the very thing she wanted to avoid ended up happening.*

The workplace is a treasure trove for the law of unintended consequences: the solution to a problem can create so many new problems that you wish you had the old one back. You yearn for the good old days, when you'd complain every day about an issue that, in hindsight, seems laughably trivial.

We can learn two things from this law. First, don't expect too much from your interventions; second, something unexpected is bound to happen.

WRONG, BUT STRONG

The law of unintended consequences: when a city profits from a construction error.

THE IKEA EFFECT: WE LIKE SOMETHING MORE IF WE'VE HAD A HAND IN IT

For a few moments, when you've finally managed to assemble that IKEA wardrobe, you bask in the glow of your craftsmanship – forgetting that all you did was put in a few screws, as millions have done before you.

Experiments by economist Michael Norton and his team have showed that the IKEA effect is a very real phenomenon. But it only happens when you've put together the furniture successfully – nothing is more frustrating than being unable to make sense of the instructions.

There is no conclusive explanation for the IKEA effect, but Norton and his colleagues believe we value a product more if we've had a hand in creating it. IKEA's creative director, Marcus Engman, told us: 'I often visit people at home to find out how our customers use our products. Once, I visited a young woman in New York who was in the process of furnishing her first apartment. Among other things, she had one of our coffee tables where you just have to screw the legs into the top. She beamed at me and said, "I made this." It's a bit silly, obviously, but when we put something like that together we inadvertently achieve something: we create a relationship between us and the object.' What do we learn from this?

Something truly fundamental: that making an effort instead of sitting back can bring a little happiness into your life.

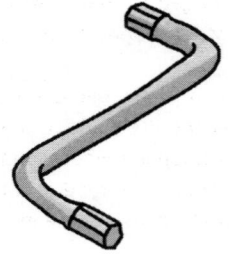

The key to happiness

THE MAYA PRINCIPLE: THE DESIGNER'S RULE

Raymond Loewy (1893–1986) had a remarkable instinct for what people like. He came up with some of the most famous designs in western culture, including the Lucky Strike pack, the Shell logo and the Greyhound bus. He had a revolutionary approach to his work, and if your job too has anything to do with design, then you should know about it.

Loewy believed that consumers are influenced by 'two opposing factors: attraction to the new and resistance to the unfamiliar'. In writing about Loewy's approach, journalist Derek Thompson calls these opposing forces 'neophilia, a curiosity about new things; and neophobia, a fear of anything too new.' Loewy called the sweet spot between the new and the familiar MAYA:

Most advanced yet acceptable.

We may crave novelty, but no matter how useful a design is, if it's *too* modern or different, our desire for the new will be overshadowed by our discomfort with the unknown. The art therefore lies in creating not a ground-breaking design, but one that is new while still being somehow familiar.

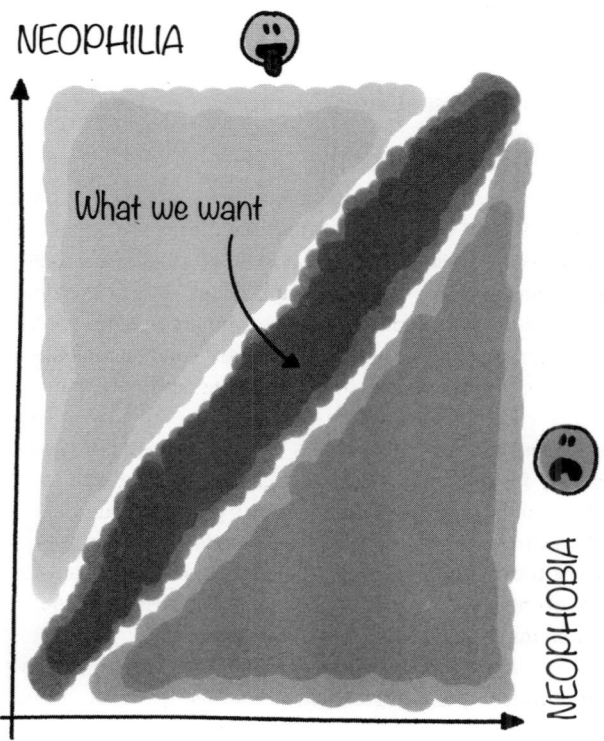

Most advanced yet acceptable.

Loewy worked intuitively – he was no scientist – but success proved him right. In 1968, psychologist Robert Zajonc from the University of Michigan tested MAYA out with an experiment (as described by Derek Thompson in *Hit Makers*): he showed participants Mandarin-style characters that supposedly represented adjectives, and asked them which they found most positive. What he discovered was that the more often a character was shown to the test subjects, the more positively they responded to it.

This is called the mere-exposure effect. Many studies have been done on it, and the findings are always the same: we prefer familiar landscapes, shapes, products and faces, while rejecting the different and unusual. One of the most obvious examples can be seen at gigs, where fans – to the act's great chagrin – keep requesting the same old hits.

But familiarity breeds contempt, and at some point even our favourite songs can sound boring. We want something that's new but not too dissimilar from the old stuff. Something that is 'most advanced yet acceptable'. This demonstrates not only our longing for the familiar and aversion to being bored, but also that we don't like it when too many people, or the wrong kind of people, like the same things as us. 'Trending' is just another word for 'dead'. It is a very fine line, though: we want to belong, but also to be individuals. We want to hear the songs we loved in our youth – just not all the time. We want to discover new things, but get upset when we find them. We enjoy the safety that familiarity brings and dream of new adventures.

But what if the new isn't any good? With the next law, we'll look at our ambivalent relationship with change from a rather different perspective.

LINDY'S LAW: SOME THINGS NEVER CHANGE

A new smartphone, a new series, a new lover ... we are constantly on the lookout for something new that promises more than what we already have. Novelty is a double-edged sword: on the one hand, it fills us with delight and claims our attention; on the other hand, it can lead to the fallacy that new is always better. In some cases, of course, it's true: a brand new computer will probably be faster and more powerful, and no one misses floppy disks these days (see Murphy's Law). But not every new idea or product is an improvement on the tried and tested. If you think about it, something that endures has often already been around for a long time, during which it has proved itself useful.

Take polyester fleece: for thousands of years, we'd used wool to keep out the cold, but in the 1970s someone invented a synthetic material to do the same thing. The revolution was short-lived, and we now associate polyester with microplastic pollution, whereas wool has lasted the course.

This is known as Lindy's law, which made its debut in a 1964 essay by cultural critic Albert Goldman. Nassim Nicholas Taleb developed it into a comprehensive theory of viability in his 2012 book *Antifragile*.

It can be summarised thus:

The longer something has been around, the longer it will probably stay around.

Chairs won't become outdated just because they have existed for a very long time. On the contrary: because they have been tried and tested, they'll likely continue to exist in future.

How does Lindy's law apply in the workplace? Well, next time you take part in a workshop about new markets, opportunities or branding, don't ask yourself merely, 'What should we do differently? How will the world change? What will happen next?'

Also ask, 'Of all the things we do, think and use today, which will endure? What *won't* change?'

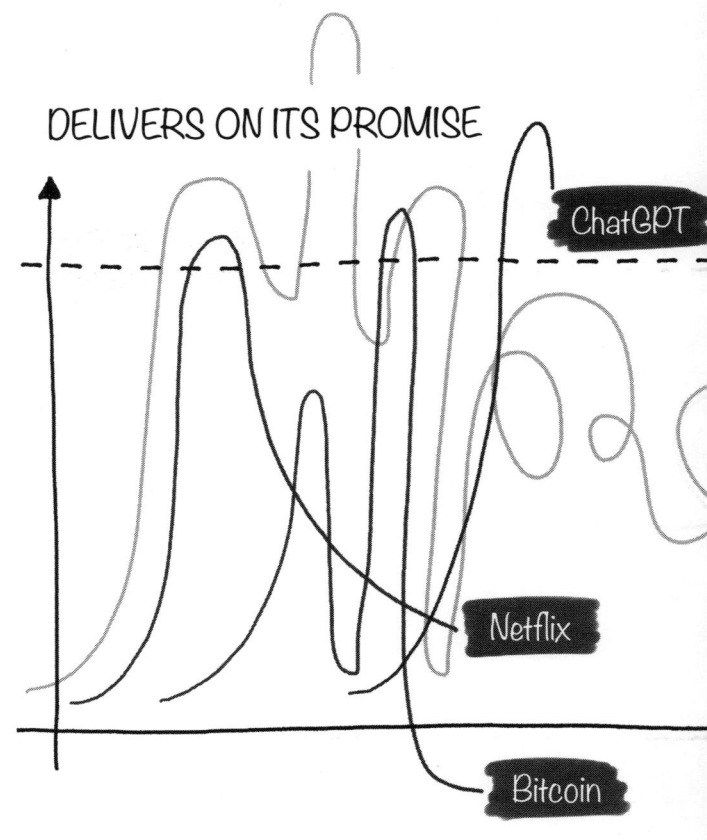

Lindy's law: The longer something has been around, the longer it will probably stay around.

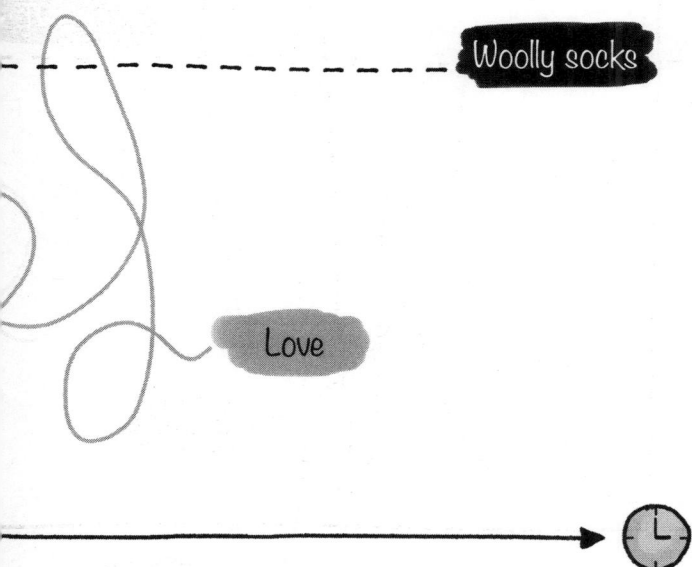

Part 3. Understanding Yourself (and Others) Better

WIIO'S LAW:
WHY WE MISUNDERSTAND EACH OTHER

Have you ever sent a text or email that the recipient took the wrong way? Have you ever tried to talk to someone who isn't listening? Have you ever given a talk no one was interested in? If so (and we're 104 per cent sure that you've answered yes to at least one of these), you will have encountered the fundamental law of communication, as formulated by Finnish academic Osmo Antero Wiio (1928–2013): *Viestintä yleensä epäonnistuu, paitsi sattumalta.* In other words:

Communication usually doesn't work, except by chance.

What he meant was that we are complicated creatures, and so clumsy and contradictory in our communications that whenever we do understand each other it's purely by accident. Wiio was joking, of course, but the popularity of his fundamental law of communication shows that there's truth in it. He then added some further tongue-in-cheek but perceptive observations, including:

'There is always someone who knows better than you what you really meant to say.'

Most of you will have felt this too, at one time or another.

According to Wiio, the reason we're constantly talking at cross purposes is that any conversation between two people is actually a complex discussion between six (!) people. They are:

1. The person you think you are
2. The person you think you're talking to
3. The person you think your interlocutor thinks you are
4. The person your interlocutor thinks they are
5. The person your interlocutor thinks you are
6. The person your interlocutor thinks you think they are.

If having a conversation is already this complicated, how can we be sure that we are expressing ourselves properly? This can lead to blaming others when communication fails. You got the wrong end of the stick, we say. You weren't listening. You were not clear. There has been a misunderstanding.

What we often forget is that it is in our power to shape and influence our communications.

Sounds complicated, but it's quite simple really: talk less, listen more. Ask questions. Don't be a know-all.

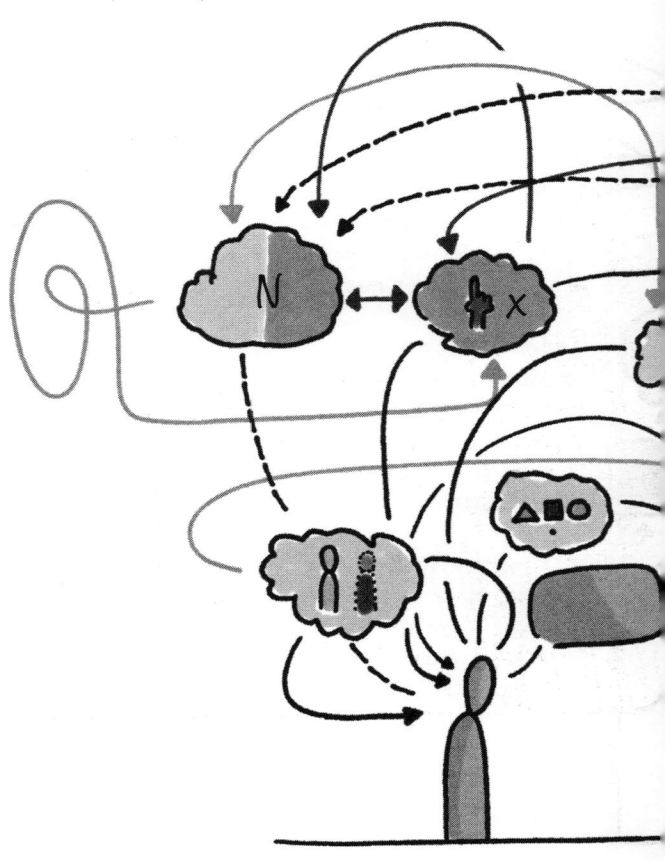

Wiio's Law: Communication usually doesn't work, except by chance.

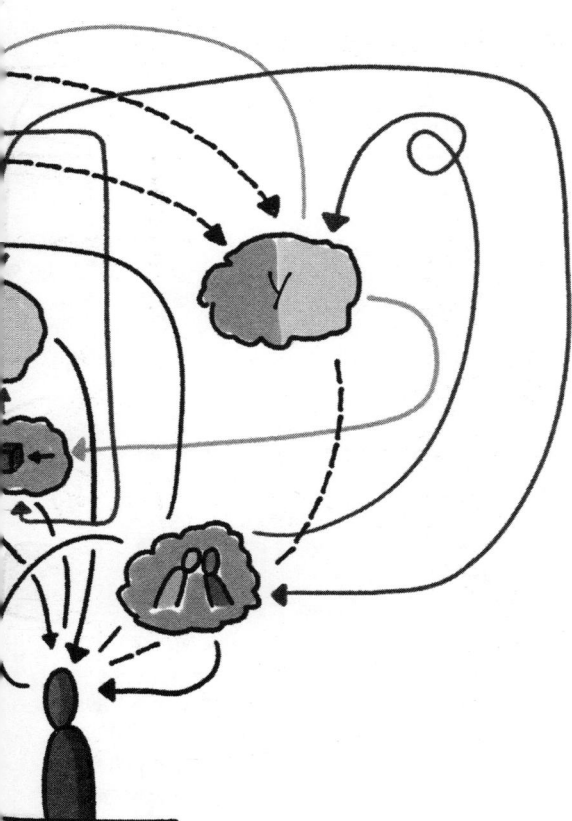

THE PETER PRINCIPLE: WHY YOUR BOSS IS INCOMPETENT

Most people think their boss is incompetent. The notion is so widespread that it even has a name: the Peter principle. It was first formulated in 1969 by Laurence Peter and Raymond Hull:

In a hierarchy, everyone tends to rise to their level of incompetence.

The Peter principle is satire, but like all good satire it contains a grain of truth.

Somebody is good at their job. They are promoted. They do well in their new role and are eventually promoted again. The process repeats itself until they land in a role that exceeds their skills: they have now reached their level of incompetence and are unfit to do the job. If we take this to its logical conclusion, then, if you work in a company where competent staff earn promotions and incompetent staff remain in their roles, at some point all leadership positions will be occupied by incompetent people.

But is it true?

In a hierarchy, everyone tends to rise to their level of incompetence.

In 2019, three researchers – Alan Benson, Danielle Li and Kelly Shue – published what appears to be the first empirical study of the Peter principle, based on 50,000 sales associates working across 200 companies. Their rather eye-opening finding was that, on average, the 1,500 staff who were promoted over the course of the study didn't turn out to be particularly good managers. They were given their new jobs based on merit (which *seems* sensible), not based on their skills (which *would be* sensible). When a top sales associate moved into a leadership role, what had qualified them for their previous job – good salesmanship – was not what they needed as a manager. In fact, by promoting them, the companies merely gained a bad manager and lost a good sales associate.

This is how you can apply the rule:

1. **If you are offered a promotion**. Think carefully about whether to accept. It is important to be self-aware and know which positions suit your skill set and which don't. Where is *your* level of incompetence?

2. **If you have a good boss.** Don't quit your job! Good managers are as rare as white Christmases.

3. **If you want to promote someone.** Consider drawing from a hat. Studies have shown that a team whose leader is appointed randomly makes smarter decisions than one that chooses its leader democratically or based on current performance. The reason for this is that whoever is chosen automatically *feels* chosen. Their colleagues' vote of confidence goes to their head, and they

start thinking about their career rather than the task in hand. But if someone is picked at random, that person has a greater sense of responsibility and tries harder to do a good job.

JASPERS' LAW: WHY WE'RE OFTEN DISAPPOINTED BY OUR BOSSES

It is a truth universally acknowledged that we are always somehow unhappy with our bosses (see the Peter principle on the previous page). They don't do what we think they should do, don't behave how we think they should behave, and don't perform as we think they should perform. Usually, we're just annoyed; sometimes, we're angry; at times even resigned. We complain and roll our eyes. But deep down, what we are is disappointed: we hoped for one thing, and got another.

We're all familiar with disappointment. Each of us has, at some time in our life, been let down, as well as let down others – two very different experiences, but neither is pleasant. What should you do when people don't live up to your expectations? And how do you deal with a boss who isn't very good?

Here's a rule that can help:

If you treat people as if they were better than they are, they will become better people.

This rule is usually attributed to philosopher Karl Jaspers (1882–1969), but we couldn't find it anywhere in his

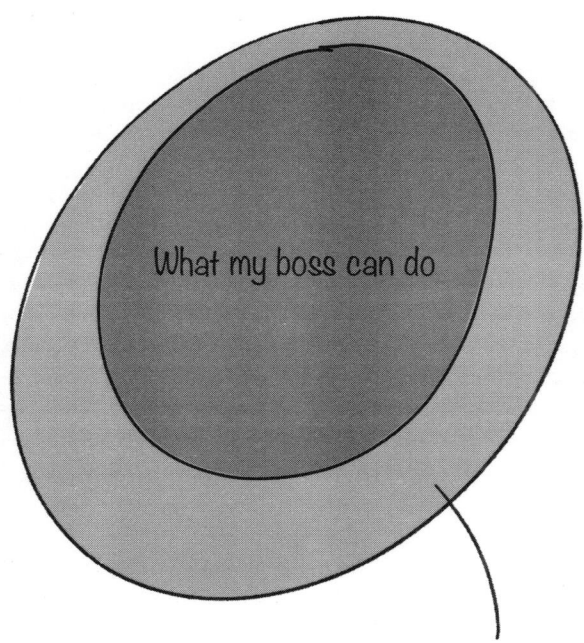

Jaspers' law: If you treat people as if they were better than they are, they will become better people.

writings (Goethe wrote something similar in *Wilhelm Meister's Apprenticeship*, though). Still, it's a great quote – and a true one.

Jaspers' law is often interpreted as a self-fulfilling prophecy for managers: if you act towards your (not-so-good) employees as if they were great at their job, you will hopefully boost their self-confidence, and eventually they'll improve.

However, we like the idea of applying it bottom-up rather than top-down. So, going back to your disappointing boss: how about dealing with them as if they were the kind of boss you wish they were? Take a moment here and think about how you act towards people you respect, value, like, are glad to have around – maybe even try to recall a good boss you've had in the past. How do you behave when they're in the room?

Of course, when you try to imagine that your boss is how they (in your view) ought to be, and treat them accordingly, what changes is not them so much as you. You'll start acting differently towards them. The changes will be very small: maybe you're slightly more relaxed, cheerful or open. Maybe you listen more closely, and are more willing to speak your mind, be more direct with your criticism. And *that's* what ends up changing them.

Sure, it's a performance. You'll need to do some pretending. But you're acting a part not to win someone's approval, but to change your own attitude. What the other person will notice is not your performance, but a shift in the atmosphere around you, which in turn will hopefully create a shift in their attitude.

Most importantly, Jaspers' law suggests that there is a better version of all of us – including you and me.

You don't have to like everything your boss does. But if you're a tad more generous towards them, you'll give them an opportunity to become a better version of themselves.

BRACH'S LAW: DON'T BELIEVE EVERYTHING YOU THINK

A woman is at the airport. It's been a long day. She buys a pack of biscuits at a café and looks around. All the tables are occupied, so she sits down at a stranger's table and starts reading her book. After a few minutes, she opens the pack, takes out a biscuit and eats it. The stranger briefly looks up, surprised, and also takes a biscuit. The woman is astonished. The cheek of him! she thinks. But she doesn't say anything, because she doesn't want to start a conversation. A little while later, she takes another biscuit – and so does he. Eventually, there's just one biscuit left. The man reaches for it, hesitates, snaps it in two and offers half to the woman. He then gets up and heads for the gate. The woman stares after him, speechless. Shortly after, her flight is called and she too goes to the gate. When she reaches into her bag to retrieve her boarding pass, she discovers a pack of biscuits. As it turns out, she'd been eating the man's biscuits all along.

There are several versions of this anecdote – Douglas Adams claims that it once happened to him – but we heard this one from Tara Brach, a psychologist and Buddhist teacher. Brach used it to illustrate the idea that we should now and again remember to 'wake up from our thoughts'. Meaning: don't forget that what you see in your mind's eye are merely thoughts. Thinking and reflection are important. Just don't believe everything you think.

Don't believe your thoughts.

This insight may not be new, but it's worth reminding ourselves of it at times, not least in the workplace. Many (though by no means all) of our troubles and fears play out *only* in our thoughts. That does not mean they aren't real – they definitely are – but when we give our thoughts free rein, we tend to focus on stuff that gets us down; which is then blown out of proportion and seems worse than it is. It's a very human thing to do.

Brach counters this with a single question:

Is it true?

This isn't another way of saying, 'You're only imagining things!' It's a serious question she asks her clients – and which we should ask ourselves too. Is what you think true? Are things *really* how you think they are? It's a powerful question, and rather than dispel all doubt, it seeds doubt. Doubt, that is, about our own assumptions.

The art of dealing with self-optimisation's contradictions.

THE LAW OF THE COMFORT ZONE: BLACK ICE OR UNCHARTED TERRITORY?

'Outside your comfort zone is where the magic happens.' It's a familiar idea – you come across it everywhere online, in self-help guides or in therapy sessions. It means that sometimes we have to put up with discomfort to create something special. When we are too comfortable, when we have replaced challenges with routines and new experiences with, say, watching Netflix, we stop developing.

On the one hand.

On the other hand, if we're honest, we too often feel like we're teetering on the brink of a nervous breakdown. Life, work, trying to be and do everything everywhere all at once ... at some point, we're bound to hit a brick wall. Could it be down to the fact that rather than leaving our comfort zone too rarely, we leave it too often?

Sometimes the magic happens inside the comfort zone.

We often venture into situations in which we feel insecure, overwhelmed, off balance. We do it because we want to grow. But when we feel insecure, overwhelmed and off balance, we turn into the opposite of what we actually want to be. We become narrow-minded, not generous; sceptical, not open; distracted, not focused; and hard-hearted rather than happy.

The point is not to avoid anything that's difficult or requires effort, but to ask whether feeling safe won't in fact help make you a better person. If our comfort zone is the place where we feel most competent and comfortable, it is also the place where we can better gauge a situation, make clear-headed decisions and be more forthcoming towards other people. We can relax there, and be more open and brave. It gives us the energy we need to help others.

Sometimes, it's good to leave familiar terrain and experience new things. Indeed, it does us no end of good. But sometimes the really brave decision – at work, at home, with family and friends – is not to try out new things but to stick with the old. To stick with it and work on it. Until the magic happens.

WHERE THE MAGIC HAPPENS

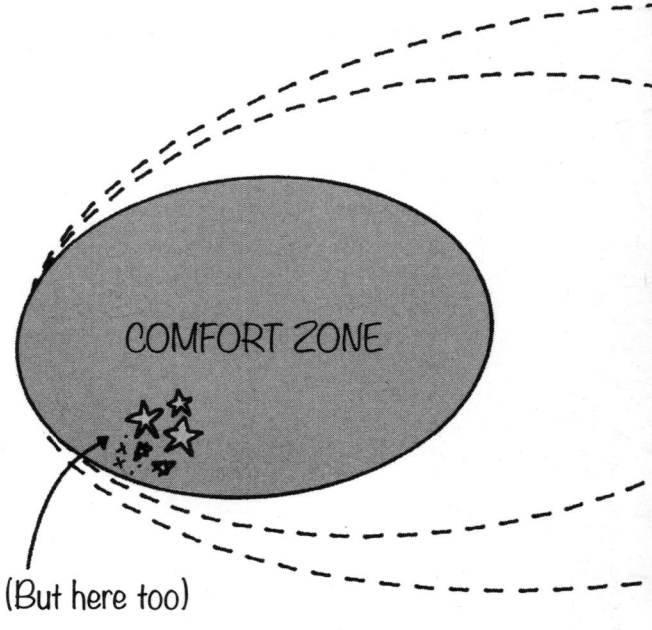

Sometimes the magic happens inside your comfort zone.

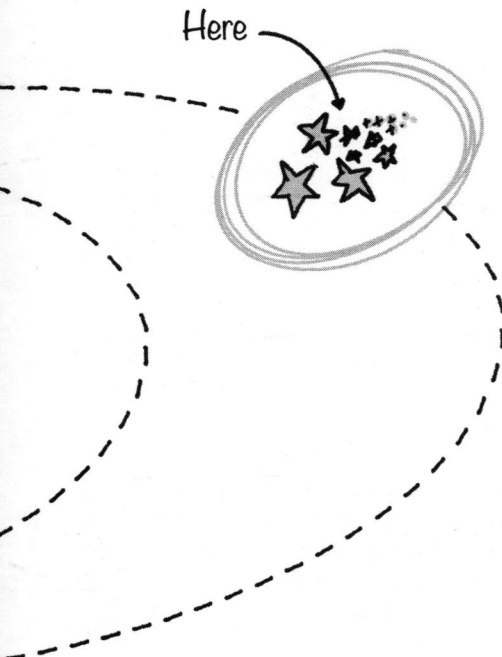

THE REGION-BETA PARADOX: SOMETIMES IT'S GOOD FOR THINGS TO BE BAD

Imagine this:

Your knee hurts a lot, and you're frustrated. You can't walk more than a short distance and stairs are a problem too – but you're also thinking that it could probably be worse. You're neither very happy nor truly unhappy.

Or how about this:

You're in an OK relationship. You like and respect each other, but you think perhaps it's not really working out. Maybe you're only staying together out of habit, so to speak, because it's what you know, or because of the kids. You're neither properly happy nor really unhappy.

Or this:

You have a job you don't particularly enjoy, but you need the money, and the routine is good for you. If you're honest, this isn't how you imagined work would be, but your boss is all right and the commute isn't bad. You're neither happy nor unhappy.

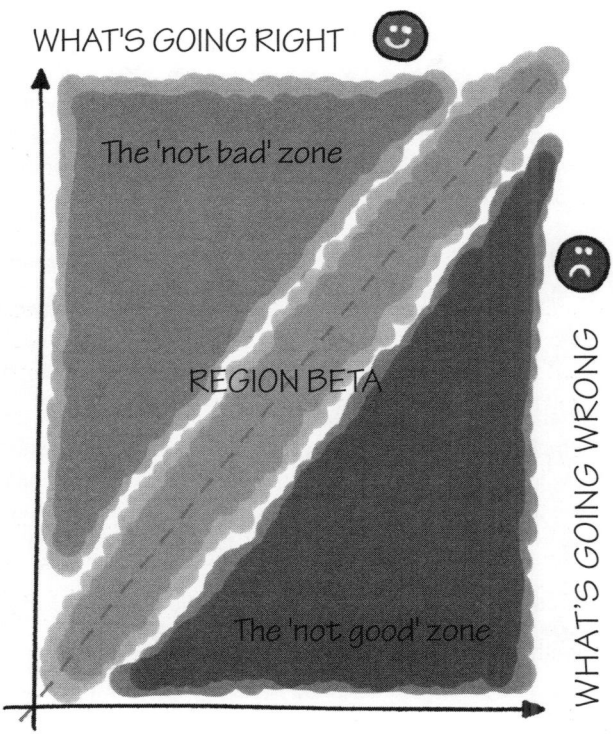

If things were worse, we'd change them.

If you find yourself in a situation like this, you are experiencing the Region-Beta paradox:

It would be better if things were worse – because then we'd do something about it.

The Region-Beta paradox was conceived in 2004 by a team of psychologists led by Daniel Gilbert. They defined it as the region where, in the long run, minor annoyances distress us more than serious issues, because we don't do anything about them.

We think the situation is not bad enough to warrant changing. In other words: we have settled for mediocrity.

And therein lies the paradox.

When things are really bad, we are more likely to ask for help, to make an effort to fix them, to turn our lives upside down. However, when they are not *that* bad we usually don't take any steps to improve the situation, and instead tolerate the middlingness of it all. We settle for Region Beta.

We can learn two things from this (and the second unfortunately contradicts the first):

1. Act.
   When something isn't right, when there is an aspect of your life you don't like, don't wait until it gets worse or fixes itself. Look for a way to improve or change things right away.

2. Wait.

What the Region-Beta paradox tells us is not that you should turn your life upside down the moment you feel dissatisfied or your knee starts creaking, but to work out when to best make a change – and when to wait.

THE GOLDILOCKS PRINCIPLE: HOW TO FIND THE MIDDLE

Have you ever been on edge, perhaps even felt stressed – but in a good way? Have you ever been anxious about an exam or a project, but also felt motivated and energised by it?

Back in 1908, psychologists Robert Yerkes and John Dodson noticed a correlation between the strength of a stimulus – our or other people's expectations, for instance – and the quality of our performance. When we are free of expectation and there are no demands placed on us, we tend to perform badly. However, unrealistic expectations also have a negative effect on performance, because they lower our self-esteem and thus our self-confidence. If the level of expectation is just right, though, we take the task before us seriously without feeling overwhelmed: the challenge is great enough to extend ourselves, but not so great as to put us off trying.

This is called the Goldilocks zone, after the fairy tale in which a girl called Goldilocks eats three different bowls of porridge, one of which is too cold, one too hot, and the third just right. In some ways, life is like a bowl of porridge:

The key is finding the right balance between too hot and too cold.

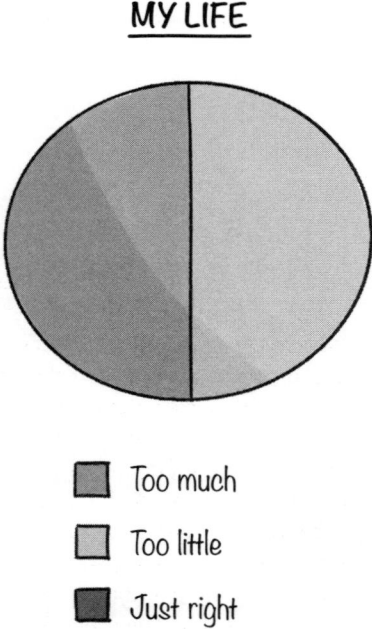

Life beyond the middle.

The Goldilocks zone applies more or less everywhere:

- Students who are afraid to fail tend to do badly in exams – as do overconfident ones.

- If you don't trust your staff and so constantly micromanage them, you'll stifle the very autonomy and responsibility you want them to display. Conversely, if you leave your staff entirely to their own devices, they may work towards the wrong goal.

- If you beat your tennis partner 80 per cent of the time, you're making it too easy on yourself – ideally, you should partner with someone you can only beat 40–60 per cent of the time. That's the Goldilocks zone, where you have to extend yourself but are also more likely to achieve your goal.

In the workplace, it means that no matter what you're working on, look for the Goldilocks zone: focus on tasks where hard work is most likely to pay off; and don't waste time on anything that will resolve itself, or which will only drive you to despair.

Incidentally, there's a word in Swedish for this zone: *lagom*. It means something like 'not too much, not too little'. Its etymological origins are uncertain, but our favourite version is that it comes from the Vikings who, whenever they needed a break from all the pillaging, would sit by the camp fire and pass around (*laget om*) a drinking vessel.

Lagom is the Swedish recipe for success: everyone gets something, but no one gets more than others. *Lagom* is the compromise with which everyone can live. It is also the fear of being unfair to someone. You hear the word in Sweden all the time: the day might be described as *lagom* warm, or a restaurant as serving *lagom*-sized portions – just the right size.

THE BIG-FISH-LITTLE-POND EFFECT: WHY STRONG COMPETITION ISN'T ALWAYS THE BEST MOTIVATION

Most parents want to send their kids to a good school. However, some research suggests that you should do the opposite, i.e. send your child not to the best school, but to the one where they will be top in their class. This is called the big-fish-little-pond effect: we feel more motivated in underperforming environments, because when we do well we get noticed and praised.

In essence, it means that we measure our value not in comparison with the rest of the world, but only in comparison with our immediate environment. When we perform better than those around us, our self-esteem increases, even if the standard is not particularly high. Conversely, if we do worse than everyone else around us, it negatively affects our self-esteem, self-efficacy and motivation – even if our performance is excellent compared with that of many other people. It isn't always true, of course: some people improve in challenging settings, and love competing against someone who's better.

Next time you find yourself having to make such a decision, ask yourself:

Do I want to stand out in a weak crowd, or be part of a strong team?

THE CLOTHES-CHAIR PRINCIPLE: WHY TIDYING UP IS GOOD FOR US

Do you have a 'clothes chair' in your bedroom, where you deposit clothes you've worn but which don't need washing yet? A chair where yesterday's clothes can rest a little, before being drafted back into service? Wearing the same thing to work two days running isn't a great idea (people are bound to notice), but you can probably wear the outfit again in a couple of days, or combine that top with a different pair of trousers, say, before consigning it to the laundry basket.

The problem with the pile of clothes on that chair is that it keeps growing. The more clothes are on the chair, the greater the probability that you put more clothes on top. It is a universal principle that can be summed up as follows:

The messier the world around me, the messier I am.

If you don't wash up straight after a meal, the sink soon becomes overwhelmed with dirty dishes. If you start leaving documents on your desk instead of filing them away, your desk will disappear among all the paper. And once you start chucking your clothes on a chair instead of putting them away, the situation in your bedroom will quickly get out of hand. Tidy desk, tidy mind. As Marie Kondo's philosophy suggests, if your room is cluttered, so is your heart.

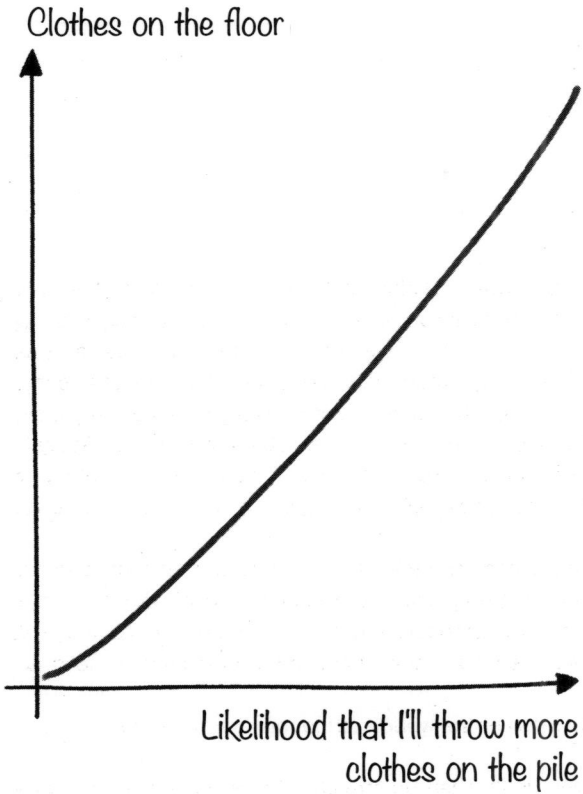

The messier the world around me, the messier I am.

Part 4. How to Handle Life's Big Questions

MORRISON'S LAWS: YOU ARE MORE THAN YOUR JOB

Shortly before her death, US author Toni Morrison (1931–2019) wrote an essay for the *New Yorker* about work. In 'The work you do, the person you are', Morrison shares the knowledge her father imparted when she got her first job. Her take (or rather, her father's take) on wage work hasn't yet entered common parlance as a 'rule' or 'principle', but we think it should.

Here, then, are Morrison's four laws of work:

1. Whatever the work is, do it well – not for the boss but for yourself.
2. You make the job; it doesn't make you.
3. Your real life is with us, your family.
4. You are not the work you do; you are the person you are.

These four points make it abundantly clear that what matters is dedication, setting limits, belonging and loving yourself.

I am not my job.

PASCAL'S WAGER: WHY BELIEVING IN GOD MIGHT NOT BE A BAD IDEA

Blaise Pascal (1623–1662) was much preoccupied by one of the biggest questions of his time: does God exist? He quickly determined that if you believe in God you don't need proof – and if you don't believe in God, nothing in the world will convince you otherwise. So he did something brilliant: instead of asking whether God exists, he asked whether it was *worth* believing in God.

If we turn this into a decision matrix, it shows two behaviour options: you believe or you don't; and two truths: there is a God, or there isn't.

1. God exists and I believe in God – I will go to heaven.
2. God does not exist and I believe in God – nothing happens.
3. God exists and I don't believe in God – I will go to hell.
4. God does not exist and I don't believe in God – nothing happens.

What it shows is that it may not be logical to believe in God, but it isn't necessarily a bad idea either. This is known as Pascal's wager, and is famously one of the first ever rules to help with decision-making.

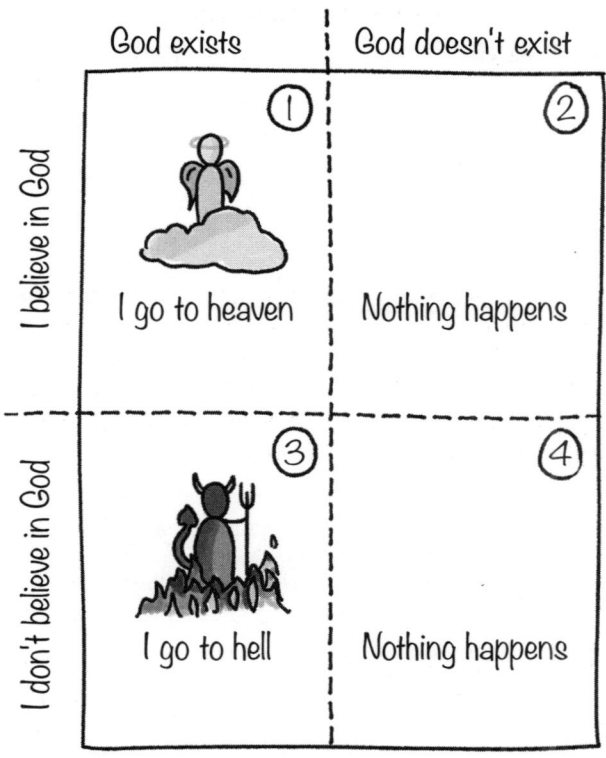

Pascal's wager: You lose nothing by believing in God – and you might hit the jackpot.

OCCAM'S RAZOR: DISTINGUISHING THE LIKELY FROM THE UNLIKELY

You're sitting on a train and suddenly realise your keys aren't in your pocket. What has happened?

1. Aliens have beamed them into a parallel universe.
2. Your dog ate them.
3. You've left them at the office.

Which is it? No. 1 is silly; no. 2 is theoretically possible, but unlikely; no. 3 is the most straightforward and plausible scenario – and probably what happened.

This is a classic example of Occam's razor (also spelled Ockham's razor), named after the Franciscan friar William of Ockham (1285–1347). You can use Occam's razor to find out what happened in any given scenario; it's a process that separates the likely from the ridiculous (as if done with a razorblade). Whether William of Ockham meant it quite like that has been much debated, but the eponymous rule is nonetheless a good one:

All other things being equal, the most straightforward explanation is probably the right one.

In other words, when there is more than one possible explanation, the one that is least complicated is also the most likely. 'Straightforward' does not mean that the explanation should be simplistic – some situations are simply not simple, but complex – but that it consists of few variables and assumptions. A more precise translation of the Latin '*Entia non sunt multiplicanda praeter necessitatem*' might be:

Entities should not be unnecessarily multiplied.

That is to say: think carefully before adding complexity to a situation.

Occam's razor is not a law, but a tool that – used properly and at the right time – saves time and energy and helps us avoid endless discussions.

Has an alien nicked my keys? Has my dog eaten them? Or did I leave them at the office? Probably the third option.

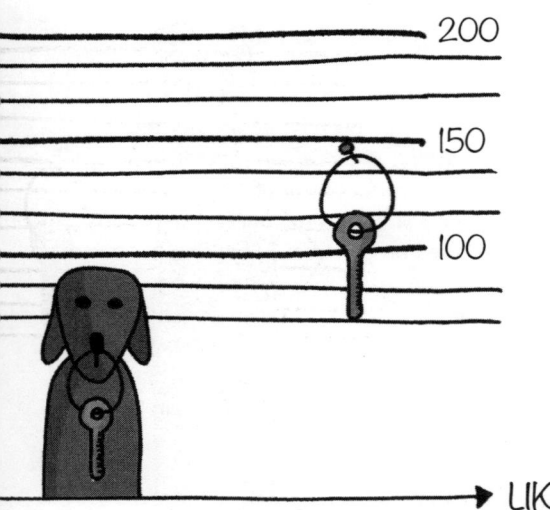

AGNES ALLEN'S LAW: WHY IT'S EASIER TO START THAN TO STOP

Historian Frederick Lewis Allen once came up with the following bon mot: 'Everything is more complicated than it looks to most people.' It's perfectly true: when you glance at something superficially, you think you understand it; but on closer inspection, even an apparently very simple case can turn out tricky.

Agnes Rogers Allen (1893–1986) was Frederick Allen's wife. She gave what he said some further thought, and came up with a better way to express reality – and in fewer words:

Almost anything is easier to get into than out of.

Clearly, what she said here applies to almost any area of life. It's easier to:

- get into a discussion than end it
- accumulate debt than pay it off
- start wars than make peace
- catch a cold than get rid of it
- gain a couple of pounds than lose them
- hurt someone than apologise
- conceive a child than give birth

- have an idea than implement it
- win a title than defend it
- subscribe than cancel your subscription
- say yes than say no
- start a list than finish it.

Of course, as always with such things, the opposite also applies: it's certainly harder to get into than out of Berlin's Berghain nightclub, and harder to blow up a balloon than to let the air out again. But all in all, Agnes Allen came up with a law that's easy to remember and very hard to forget.

Agnes Allen's Law: Almost anything is easier to get into than out of.

KORZYBSKI'S LAW: THE MAP IS NOT THE TERRITORY

In his complex magnum opus *Science and Sanity*, equally complex mathematician and philosopher Alfred Korzybski (1879-1950) discusses the map-territory problem, which stipulates that there are two worlds: the world of language (the map) and that of experience (the territory). In other words: a description of something is not the same as the thing itself, and our perception of reality is not the same as reality. Or:

The map is not the territory.

For example, a menu is not the same as a meal, a painting is not the object it depicts and a book about parenting cannot stand in for actually parenting a child. There is a further complication with the last example: parenting guides are *about* children, but are not *portraits of* any one particular child. Most importantly, they are not shaped by *your* child (and your child, alas, is not shaped by them). We all have different realities and circumstances.

The rules in this book are in a way also victims of the map-territory relationship: they are approaches to reality, but not reality itself. They can still be useful, but the art is knowing when they're useful for you and your circumstances – and when they're not (see Box's law, p. 162). If you are ever stuck on a problem, or a method isn't working for you in a particular situation, consider these possibilities, drawn from Korzybski's law:

1. **You're using the wrong map.** Even an excellent map of Bucharest won't help you find your way around Budapest. A screwdriver is a brilliant tool, but you can't hammer a nail into a wall with one. Ask yourself: am I looking at things the wrong way?

2. **There is more than one map.** We often think that what seems logical and helpful to us must seem logical and helpful to everyone else. It's easy to forget that there are all sorts of maps. There is more than one way out of the woods. Listen to others, be flexible and open to other methods.

3. **You are trying to use the same map for every territory.** It's tempting to fall in love with your own way of thinking, approach or solution, and subconsciously to try to fit reality to your idea of it. But a landscape will never reshape itself to match the map. Now and then, you have to get out there and inspect the lie of the land. What is the reality of the situation? And if it doesn't fit your vision of it, be ready to throw out the old idea and follow what's in front of you.

The map is not the territory.

THE LAW OF TWO SIDES: WHY NOTHING IS ALL GOOD OR ALL BAD

In a village, there once lived a wise man with his son. They had a small farmyard and a horse. The villagers said, 'What a lovely horse, you're so lucky.' The wise man replied, 'Maybe, maybe not.'

One day, the horse ran away. The villagers said, 'Your only horse – what bad luck!' The wise man replied, 'Maybe, maybe not.'

Then the horse returned, followed by two wild horses. The villagers said, 'Now you have three horses, you lucky so-and-so.' The wise man replied, 'Maybe, maybe not.' His son tried to tame the wild horses, but fell and broke his leg. The villagers said, 'Your only son – what bad luck!' The wise man replied, 'Maybe, maybe not.'

Then war broke out, and every man of fighting age was drafted. Except for the wise man's son, on account of his broken leg. The villagers said, 'We have all lost our sons, except for you – how lucky you are!' The wise man replied, 'Maybe, maybe not.'

The wise man knows that what happens to him isn't all good or all bad. Things that seem bad can turn out well in the end (and vice versa – unfortunately).

THE WAY IS THE GOAL IS IN THE WAY

There are two sides to everything.

THE 1 PER CENT RULE: WHY OUTRAGE IS POINTLESS

The big debates of our time seem to have two things in common: first, they're happening on social media; second, it feels like pretty much everyone must have chimed in by now. On this second point, though, you'd be wrong. They haven't. In fact, very few people have posted anything at all.

This observation was made by Bradley Horowitz back in 2006, when he was a director at Yahoo. He claimed that just 1 per cent of members of a given social media network post anything, 9 per cent comment on the posts of the 1 per cent, and the rest watch the spectacle unfold. His observation was much discussed, examined and refined – until it became known as the 1 per cent rule:

Out of 100 users of a social media platform, one person produces content, nine people comment or share that content, and ninety per cent just read it.

What does this tell us? It tells us that a small number of people are responsible for all that noise. So the next time you read a discussion online and wonder if the whole world has gone mad, remember the 1 per cent rule: no, we haven't all gone mad. Nine per cent of us are discussing what 1 per cent have said, but the rest just shake their heads, read it – and scroll past.

1 per cent of social media users post something, 9 per cent engage with it and 90 per cent read it.

LAVER'S LAW OF FASHION: WHAT YOUR CLOTHES SAY ABOUT YOU

In fashion, there's one simple rule:

The first and last iterations of a trend look absurd.

Let's break this down. According to Laver's law, named after fashion historian James Laver (1899–1975), fashion is cyclical and everything comes back around – eventually. He gave fashion trends the following timescale:

Indecent: 10 years before its time
Shameless: 5 years before its time
Outré (Daring): 1 year before its time
Smart: Current fashion
Dowdy: 1 year after its time
Hideous: 10 years after its time
Ridiculous: 20 years after its time
Amusing: 30 years after its time
Charming: 70 years after its time

It takes around fifty years, said Laver, for a trend to come back into fashion. More recent studies have shown that the fashion cycle has shortened to roughly twenty years. The lesson we take away from Laver's law is this: there's no right or wrong – only 'too late' or 'too early'.

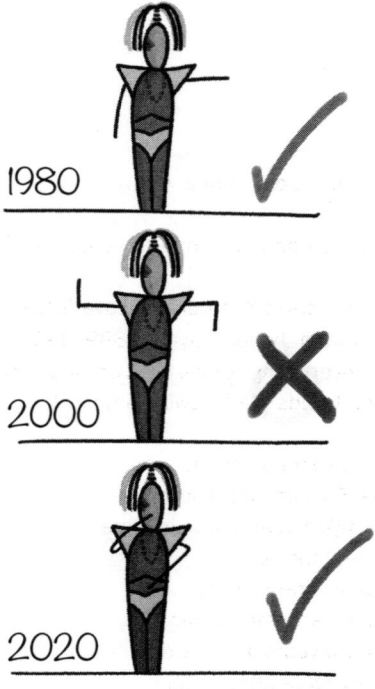

Fashion comes and goes. And comes back. And goes again.

THE POPSICLE TEST: SHOULD I MOVE?

'Am I living in the right place?' We've all asked ourselves that question at some point. The only way to truly answer it is by moving elsewhere, but fortunately there's a little thought experiment to help you assess the situation. Think of where you live now, and ask yourself:

Can an eight-year-old safely walk to the ice cream shop, buy an ice cream and get back home before it melts?

If so, you're living in the right place. If not, you should move.

This is the famous 'popsicle test'. We don't know who first came up with it, but it's been doing the rounds of urban planning presentations and parenting blogs for years now. Think of it as a tastier version of the 15-minute-city concept. It shortens the whole tiring pros-and-cons process, and has a clever premise at its centre – i.e. that what's good for children is good for everyone else.

After all, what are the important factors when it comes to choosing a place to live? Location, location, location. But what does 'location' mean? That house prices in the area will go up in the next twenty years? No: 'location' means that the area is safe enough for kids to be out and about on their own. And that there's a lovely ice cream shop nearby.

The popsicle test: more reliable than estate agents.

THE TOCQUEVILLE EFFECT: WHY OUTCRIES HAPPEN WHEN THINGS ARE ALREADY IMPROVING

Remember the 1 per cent rule? When you scroll through social media, it's easy to get the impression that everyone is outraged by something. Wherever you look, there's rage, accusations, outcries. The world seems off-kilter somehow, and there's a lot of division. 'Togetherness' has become a foreign word. But hang on – what if the opposite were true? What if all that outrage were a sign that there's *more* fairness and justice than before?

This idea has been posited among others by Alexis de Tocqueville, in his 1835 book *Democracy in America*. Tocqueville had travelled across the US for ten months, in order to compile a report for the French government about how a fairer, more democratic society affects a country's population. In the course of this trip, he made an observation now known as the Tocqueville effect, and which social psychologists describe thus:

As a society becomes fairer, people become more sensitive to the remaining inequalities.

In other words: revolution happens not when a society is at its most unjust, but when the injustice is already on the wane.

One explanation for this is that when your interests are routinely ignored or even considered illegal, it is damned difficult – sometimes even dangerous – to point out an injustice, criticise the status quo or demand change. It is only when your interests are starting to be acknowledged that you might have the courage to speak up. In other words, the brave few who challenged the status quo early on have laid the groundwork, and have had an effect: the culture has shifted, more people are aware of the issues, and more people are willing to speak up or join the fight as allies.

And now for the paradox. When we witness a group of people being ignored, it seems to us that we must live in a seriously unjust world. What it might really show, though, is that we are getting closer to a more just world. Those people's needs are more widely understood – which is how we're able to know that they are being ignored in the first place. Hopefully, it also means that steps are being taken to do something about it.

The Tocqueville effect shows that outrage doesn't necessarily mean things are worse than they used to be. Rather, it can be taken as a sign that we have made progress in the fight for a fairer, more inclusive society.

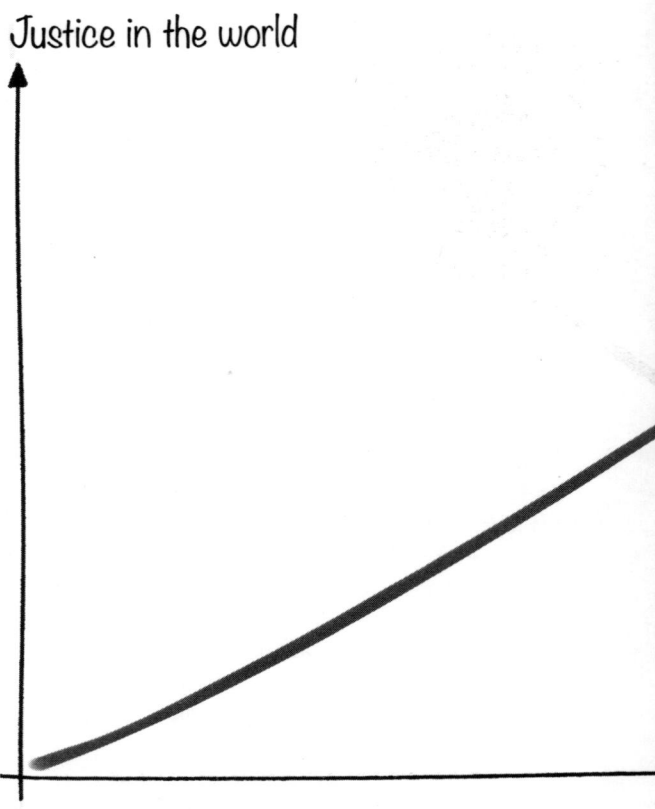

The less injustice there is, the more sensitive we are to the injustice that remains.

Tocqueville effect

How unjust the world feels

THE ONE-STEP-CLOSER RULE: HOW TO BEHAVE, GENERALLY SPEAKING

One day, Sheikh Abu Sa'id, an eleventh-century Muslim mystic, came to Tous. In anticipation of his sermon, so many faithful followers streamed into the mosque that soon there was barely any room left. 'Come a step closer, all of you, wherever you are,' said the event organiser. The sheikh heard him, and when his turn came to speak he announced that his sermon would no longer be taking place; the organiser had already said everything that he, Abu Sa'id, had wanted to say. It echoed the wisdom of other, older sages:

Everyone, wherever you are, come one step closer. This is how everything changes.

He then stepped off the stage and didn't say another word that day.

This story was recently retold by Navid Kermani in *Come a Little Closer, All of You, Wherever You Are*; and we believe that it can be understood as a sort of universal law applying to all conflicts, personal or professional:

Both sides need to take a step away from their convictions, and a step towards each other.

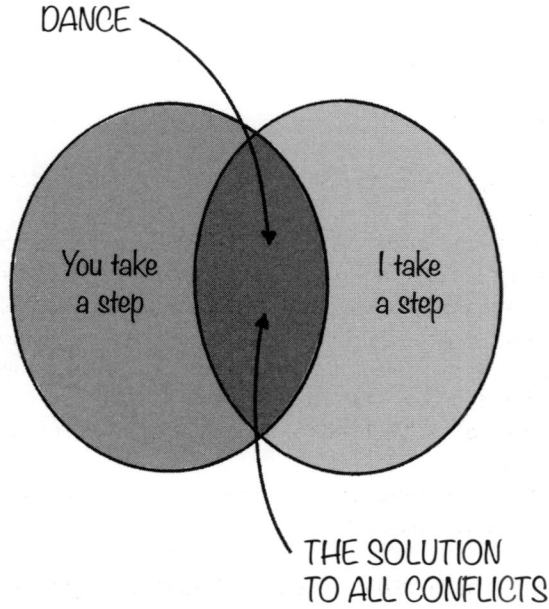

Coming a step closer means leaving your convictions a little.

THE 10-10-10 METHOD: HOW TO STOP WORRYING ABOUT DECISIONS

The art of decision-making is not always about how to arrive at the *right* decision (no one knows the answer to that, not even the authors of this book), but instead it can be about how to cope with the possibility that you might make the *wrong* one.

Business advisor Suzy Welch once came up with a rule of thumb to help us be more relaxed about decision-making. Any time you find yourself needing to choose between two options and unsure which is the right one, ask yourself these three questions:

1. What will I think of my decision in ten minutes' time?
2. What will I think of my decision in ten months' time?
3. What will I think of my decision in ten years' time?

Take a moment to answer these three questions properly. What you are doing is considering the choice you have to make from the perspective of the future. You are looking at the short-, medium- and long-term consequences of your decision, and taking away some of the scariness in the process.

Before making an important decision, ask yourself how you'll feel about it in ten minutes, ten months and ten years.

Epilogue

BOX'S LAW:
HOW TO APPLY THE RULES IN THIS BOOK

The principles, laws, paradoxes, effects and rules that we have presented in our little book, dear reader, differ from real rules and laws in a few crucial ways.

Real ones, such as the rules of a game, are something you have to stick to. They apply all the time, and tell you what you are and are not allowed to do, what is right and what is wrong. The rules in this book are a different animal. They apply often – but not always. They are valid in certain situations – but not all. In themselves, they are nothing: you have to use them, try them out – but also question, adapt and set them aside.

There is even a great rule about how we should handle rules like this. It is called Box's law, after statistician George E. P. Box (1919–2013):

All models are wrong, but some are useful.

What does it mean? Let's look at its individual components. The first part – *'All models are wrong'* – is a nod to the nit-pickers and pedants. If you look long enough, everything can seem wrong.

The second part of the sentence is the crucial bit: '*but some are useful*'. What Box is saying is that models justify their existence not because sometimes they *don't* help, but because sometimes they *do*. As Mark Manson once said, 'A little bit of truth exists in everything; but the whole truth in nothing.'

According to George Box, if all models are wrong, the specific question we must ask is, how wrong can they be before they stop being useful altogether? There will always be a discrepancy between model and reality: the map is not the territory (see p. 140), the CV is not the person, the diagnosis is not the patient. What matters is how much discrepancy is acceptable in terms of your undertaking. Is there any way in which the model can still help, despite its flaws? In other words: take what you can, and leave the rest.

The image on the next page applies this idea to an everyday scenario. Clearly, we should judge a tool not by its precision, but by its ability to help us solve the problem we are facing at that particular moment.

HOW TO OPEN A BOTT

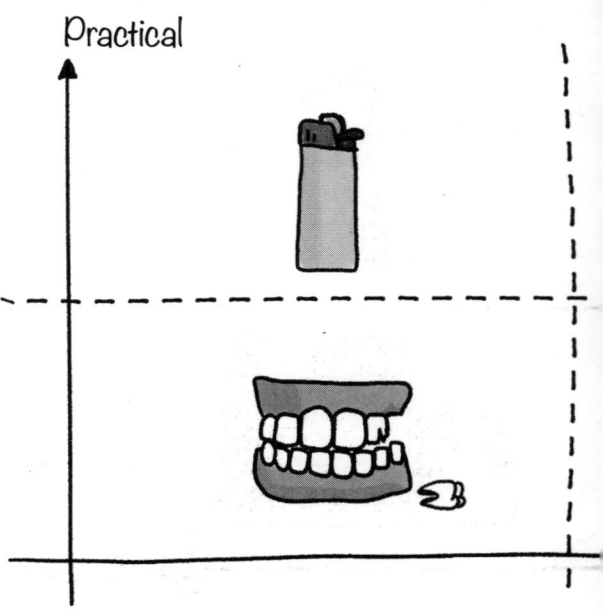

'There is no right and wrong. What matters is whether the beer bottle is open. People who try to sabotage everything with words aren't interested in having a beer with you.' Jens Bachmann

OF  BEER

 Precise

MORE RULES:
SOME OTHER THINGS THAT ARE TRUE

The list of (un)written laws and (un)known rules is endless, and this book naturally only contains a small selection of them. Here are a few more of our favourites. Some may seem in jest at first, but the more you think about it them, the more profound they become.

The law of the instrument:
It is tempting, if the only tool you have is a hammer, to treat everything as if it were a nail.

Cunningham's law:
The best way to find the right answer online is not to ask a question; it's to post the wrong answer.

Gall's law:
A complex system that works is invariably found to have evolved from a simple system that worked. A complex system designed from scratch never works and cannot be patched up to make it work.

Putt's law:
Technology is dominated by two types of people: those who understand what they do not manage and those who manage what they do not understand.

Clarke's law:
When a distinguished but elderly scientist states that something is possible, they are almost certainly right. When they state that something is impossible, they are very probably wrong.

Betteridge's law of headlines:
Any headline that ends in a question mark can be answered by the word 'no'.

Barth's distinction:
There are two kinds of people in this world: those who distinguish between two kinds of people, and those who don't.

Boob's law:
It's always in the last place you look.

Appendix

SOURCES

The Ketchup Effect
With thanks to Jeppe Hansgaard, CEO of Innovisor, whose LinkedIn post gave us the idea. *Tak skal du have!*
Our example of the power of followers comes from this TED talk by Derek Sivers: 'How to start a movement', February 2010, www.ted.com/talks/derek_sivers_how_to_start_a_movement

Sturgeon's Law
There are different versions of what Theodore Sturgeon supposedly said when and where. See sfdictionary.com/view/328/sturgeons-law

Parkinson's Law
C. Northcote Parkinson, *Parkinson's Law: Or the Pursuit of Progress* (John Murray, 1958).

The 333 Method
From Oliver Burkeman's newsletter, *The Imperfectionist*, '3/3/3, a method for structuring the day', ckarchive.com/b/e5uph7hx43mn
We also like a similar method called 1-2-3, by Greg McKeown, described in his podcast on gregmckeown.com

Hofstadter's Law
Douglas Hofstadter, *Gödel, Escher, Bach: An Eternal Golden Braid* (Basic Books, 1979).
Roger Buehler, Dale Griffin, Michael Ross, 'Exploring the "planning fallacy": Why people underestimate their task completion times', *Journal of Personality and Social Psychology*, 67(3) (1994), 366–81.

Sander Koole and Mascha van't Spijker, 'Overcoming the planning fallacy through willpower: Effects of implementation intentions on actual and predicted task-completion times', *European Journal of Social Psychology*, 30(6) (2000), 873–88.

Plotz's Law
With thanks to David Plotz – welcome to the canon of useful rules! 'Before you accept any invitation ... You must ask yourself this question' was first published in *Slate* (2014, May 29), slate.com

The Pareto Principle
Vilfredo Pareto, *Manual of Political Economy* (1906).
Joseph Juran, 'Pareto Principle (80/20 Rule) & Pareto Analysis Guide', 12 March 2019, juran.com
James Clear, 'Live the Pareto Principle lifestyle', jamesclear.com/quotes

Parkinson's Law of Triviality
C. Northcote Parkinson, *Parkinson's Law: Or the Pursuit of Progress* (John Murray, 1958).

Brooks' Law
Frederick P. Brooks, *The Mythical Man-Month* (Addison-Wesley, 1975).

Goodhart's Law
Horst Siebert, *Der Kobra-Effekt: Wie man Irrwege der Wirtschaftspolitik vermeidet* (*The Cobra Effect: How to avoid mistakes in economic policy*) (Deutsche Verlags-Anstalt, 2001).

The Locksmith's Paradox
There are different versions of the story of Picasso and the locksmith. We first read it in a column by Guy Cookson-Rabouhi (thank you for the inspiration!): 'How Picasso and the Locksmiths' Paradox show time is not always money', 22 December 2016, hotfootdesign.co.uk
For Dan Ariely's encounter with a locksmith, see 'Locksmiths', 15 December 2010, danariely.com

Murphy's Law
Nick Spark, *A History of Murphy's Law* (Lulu.com, 2006).
Robert Matthews, 'Tumbling toast, Murphy's Law and the fundamental constants', *European Journal of Physics*, 16(4) (1995), 172–6.

Chesterton's Fence
G. K. Chesterton, 'The drift from domesticity', in *The Thing: Why I Am Catholic* (Dodo, Mead & Co, 1929), pp. 27–37.

Amara's Law
Roy Amara never formally published Amara's Law; the concept began appearing during the late 1970s. In 1983, he repeated it, in a slightly different wording, in an interview with John Hillkirk: 'Rate of changes clouds the future for seers', *Journal & Courier (Gannett News Service)*, 5 May 1983.

The KISS Principle
Ben R. Rich, 'Clarence Leonard (Kelly) Johnson, 1910–1990', Biographical memoir, National Academy of Sciences, 1995.

Sutton's Law
Robert Sutton, 'Sutton's Law: "If you think that you have a new idea, you are wrong. Someone probably already had it."' 4 January 2016, LinkedIn. You'll find a close analysis of the phenomenon, with examples, in Robert K. Merton's book *On the Shoulders of Giants* (Free Press, 1965).

The Canada Principle
Marc Randolph, 'The Canada Principle', marcrandolph.com

The Law of Unintended Consequences
Robert K. Merton, 'The unanticipated consequences of purposive social action', *American Sociological Review*, 1(6) (1936), 894–904.

The IKEA Effect
Michael I. Norton, Daniel Mochon and Dan Ariely, 'The IKEA Effect: When labor leads to love', *Journal of Consumer Psychology*, 22(3) (2012), 453–60.
Conversation with Marcus Engman, August 2017.

The MAYA Principle
Raymond Loewy, *Never Leave Well Enough Alone* (Simon & Schuster, 1951).
Derek Thompson, 'The four-letter code to selling just about anything', *Atlantic*, Jan/Feb 2017, theatlantic.com
Derek Thompson, *Hit Makers: The Science of Popularity in an Age of Distraction* (Penguin Books, 2017).

Lindy's Law
Nassim Nicholas Taleb, *Antifragile: Things That Gain from Disorder* (Penguin Books, 2012).

Wiio's Law
Osmo A. Wiio, *Wiion lait – ja vähän muidenkin* ('Wiio's laws – and a few others') (Weilin + Göös, 1978).

The Peter Principle
Alan Benson, Danielle Li and Kelly Shue, 'Promotions and the Peter Principle', *Quarterly Journal of Economics*, 134(4) (2019), 2085–134.
Alexander Haslam et. al., 'Inspecting the emperor's clothes: Evidence that random selection of leaders can enhance group performance', *Group Dynamics: Theory, Research, and Practice*, 2(3) (1998), 168–84.

Brach's Law
Tara Brach, 'Three core reminders for spiritual growth: Awakening mind, heart & presence', YouTube.com, 28 June 2023. www.youtube.com/watch?v=7Z05Ec0Apb8

The Region-Beta Paradox
Daniel T. Gilbert et al., 'The peculiar longevity of things not so bad', *Psychological Science*, 15(1) (2004), 14–19.

The Goldilocks Principle
Robert M. Yerkes and John D. Dodson, 'The relation of strength of stimulus to rapidity of habit-formation', *Journal of Comparative Neurology & Psychology*, 18(5) (1908), 459–82.

The Big-Fish-Little-Pond Effect
Herbert Marsh, 'The big-fish-little-pond effect on academic self-concept', *Journal of Educational Psychology*, 79(3) (1987), 280–95.
The Clothes-Chair Principle
Marie Kondo, *Spark Joy: An illustrated master class on the art of organizing and tidying up* (Ten Speed Press, 2016).

Morrison's Laws
Toni Morrison, 'The work you do, the person you are', *New Yorker*, 29 May 2017.

Pascal's Wager
Blaise Pascal, *Pensées and Other Writings* (trans. Honor Levi) (Oxford University Press, 2008).

Occam's Razor
There is no single authoritative version of Occam's rule; Johannes Clauberg's from 1654 ('*Entia non sunt multiplicanda praeter necessitatem*') is probably the most well known.

Agnes Allen's Law
Paul Dickson, *The Official Rules: 5,427 laws, principles and axioms to help you cope with crises, deadlines, bad luck, rude behavior, red tape, and attacks by inanimate objects* (Dover Publications, 2013)

Korzybski's Law
Alfred Korzybski, *Science and Sanity* (Institute of General Semantics, 1933).
See also Rhiannon Beaubien and Shane Parrish's excellent introduction to the theory in their book *The Great Mental Models. Volume 1: General Thinking Concepts* (Latticework Publishing, 2018).

The Law of Two Sides
There are various versions of the parable, and the one in the *Huainanzi* (second century BCE) is most likely the original. We found ours in Björn Natthiko Lindeblad's *Jag kan ha fel och andra visdomar från mitt liv som buddhistmunk* ('I may be wrong, and other insights from my life as a Buddhist monk') (Bonnier Fakta, 2020).
The illustration is a homage to Thomas Schöb's brilliant *Wendesätze* for Swiss Life.

The 1 Per Cent Rule
Bradley Horowitz, 'Creators, synthesizers, and consumers', blog.elatable.com, 16 February 2006.

Laver's Law of Fashion
James Laver, *Taste and Fashion: From the French Revolution Until Today* (Harrap, 1937).

The Popsicle Test
No one knows who originally came up with it, but we first heard about it in a talk by Simon Kuper at an urban planning conference in Warsaw.

The Tocqueville Effect
Alexis de Tocqueville, *Democracy in America* (trans. Arthur Goldhammer) (Library of America, 2004).

The One-Step-Closer Rule
Fritz Meier, *Abu Sa'id Abu'l-Khayr – Wirklichkeit und Legende* ('Abul Sa'id Abu'l-Khayr, the real man and the legend') (Bibliothèque Pahlavi, 1976).
Gudrun Schubert helped us trace the source, and Kambiz Shafei helped with the German translation.

The 10-10-10 Method
Suzy Welch, *10-10-10: A Life-Transforming Idea* (Simon & Schuster, 2009).

Epilogue: Box's Law
George E.P. Box, 'Robustness in the strategy of scientific model building', in R.L. Launer and G.N. Wilkinson (eds) *Robustness in Statistics* (Academic Press, 1979), pp. 201–36.
George E.P. Box and Norman Draper, *Empirical Model-Building and Response Surfaces* (Wiley, 1986).
The Mark Manson quote is from his blog, '3 principles for a better life', markmanson.net

More Rules
John Peers, *1,001 Logical Laws, Accurate Axioms, Profound Principles, Trusty Truisms, Homey Homilies, Colorful Corollaries, Quotable Quotes, and Rambunctious Ruminations for All Walks of Life* (Doubleday, 1979).

ABOUT THE AUTHORS

Mikael Krogerus is Finnish, but was born in Stockholm and is a graduate of the Kaospilot business school in Denmark. He has worked for various media, including the *Neue Zürcher Zeitung*'s *Folio* supplement, and is now editor at Zurich-based *Das Magazin*. Mikael's personal rule is 'Write It Down': after each important meeting, interesting encounter or fascinating read, briefly jot down your key takeaways. 'Briefly' meaning no more than a couple of sentences. Don't rely on your memory: if it isn't written down somewhere, it doesn't exist.

Roman Tschäppeler is Swiss and was born in Bern. Like Mikael, he is a graduate of the Kaospilot business school in Denmark, as well as of the Zurich University of the Arts. He advises foundations, corporations and teams on strategy and helps them to develop ideas. Roman's personal rule is 'Less Than Three Minutes': can you accomplish what you've been asked to do in less than three minutes? If yes, do it right away. If not, add it to your to-do list and do it at a more convenient time, alongside other similar tasks.

Together, they are the co-authors of an internationally bestselling series of smart-thinking books including *The Decision Book, The Get Things Done Book* and *The Change Book*.

www.rtmk.ch

ACKNOWLEDGEMENTS

First of all, we would like to thank the people who originally came up with the rules in this book; without their knack for putting so much into so few words, our book simply wouldn't exist.

A special thank you to Severin Bruttin for his ruthless and constructive fact-checking, and to our wonderful publishing team at Profile. Thank you also to Hanna Nilsson Zettersten, Simon Brunner, J.D. Kemming, Dag Grødal and Benno Maggi, who have supported us in countless ways all these years as sparring partners, idea-suppliers and feedback-givers. A bunch of flowers is on its way to Jens Bachmann, for his brilliant quote on p. 164, and to our LinkedIn readers: week in, week out, they draw us into multi-layered and illuminating discussions and are an endless source of inspiration. Thank you also to the members of TC Champagne, for showing the world how to live the 'That'll Do' rule; and to the whole Tagi-Magi team for their editorial support. Ethan Mollick and Bob Sutton's posts were a key source of inspiration – as was the Kaospilot School, where it all began twenty years ago.

And finally, without these two people we would not be who we are: thank you, Ondine Riesen, and thank you, Franziska Schutzbach.

First published in Great Britain in 2026 by
Profile Books Ltd
29 Cloth Fair
London
EC1A 7JQ
www.profilebooks.com

First published in 2024 in Switzerland by Kein & Aber AG Zürich

Copyright © 2024 by Kein & Aber AG Zürich – Berlin
English-language translation copyright © Gesche Ipsen, 2026
Illustrations copyright © Roman Tschäppeler

Most chapters in this book first appeared (in a shortened version) in *Das Magazin*.

10 9 8 7 6 5 4 3 2 1

Printed and bound in Great Britain by
CPI Group (UK) Ltd, Croydon CR0 4YY

The moral right of the author and the translator has been asserted.

All rights reserved. Without limiting the rights under copyright reserved above, no part of this publication may be reproduced, stored or introduced into a retrieval system, or transmitted, in any form or by any means (electronic, mechanical, photocopying, recording or otherwise), without the prior written permission of both the copyright owner and the publisher of this book.

A CIP catalogue record for this book is available from the British Library.

Our product safety representative in the EU is BGC Sustainability & Compliance, 7 avenue du Général Leclerc, Paris, 75014, France
https://baldwinglobalconsulting.com

ISBN 978 1 80522 549 2
eISBN 978 1 80522 548 5